A Council That Will Never End

Lumen Gentium
and the Church Today

Paul Lakeland

A Michael Glazier Book

LITURGICAL PRESS
Collegeville, Minnesota

www.litpress.org

A Michael Glazier Book published by Liturgical Press

Excerpts from documents of the Second Vatican Council are from *Vatican Council II: The Basic Sixteen Documents*, by Austin Flannery, OP, © 1996 (Costello Publishing Company, Inc.). Used with permission.

Scripture texts in this work are taken from the *New Revised Standard Version Bible* © 1989, Division of Christian Education of the National Council of the Churches of Christ in the United States of America. Used by permission. All rights reserved.

1   2   3   4   5   6   7   8   9

Library of Congress Cataloging-in-Publication Data

Lakeland, Paul, 1946–
     A council that will never end : Lumen gentium and the church today / Paul Lakeland.
       pages   cm
     "A Michael Glazier book."
     Includes bibliographical references and index.
     ISBN 978-0-8146-8066-7 — ISBN 978-0-8146-8091-9 (ebook)
     1. Vatican Council (2nd : 1962–1965). Constitutio dogmatica de Ecclesia.   2. Church.   3. Catholic Church—Doctrines.   I. Title.
BX1746.L285   2013
262'.02—dc23   2013018428

Contents

This book is dedicated to two of my greatest teachers,
Winifred Livesey and Arthur Malone, in gratitude.

*"It was for a mystical reason that I decided to go to St. Peter's
this morning: to participate in the grace and the occasion
of the Council at its most decisive moment."*

— Yves Congar, November 21, 1964,
the date of the promulgation of
Lumen Gentium

Preface and Acknowledgments

The problem with anniversaries is that they often focus on the past event rather than the present reality. This is less likely to be the case if the anniversary commemorates the beginning of something still very much alive. It is the difference between toasting the hundredth birthday of a favorite aunt and recognizing the anniversary of the end of the First World War. In the first case we focus on the person present in the room, in the second on an event that happened long ago. So as we begin to think about the fifty years that have elapsed since the Second Vatican Council's Constitution on the Church, *Lumen Gentium*, was ratified by the Council fathers, we need to ask ourselves if it feels more like Aunt Millie's birthday party or the bittersweet reverence for a significant but long-past moment in world history. Is *Lumen Gentium* still with us?

In the chapters that follow we will take for granted that *Lumen Gentium* is indeed still with us in a variety of ways. As a document, it will always be part of the ecclesial tradition. A thousand years from now it will still be there, and maybe still read. More important, it is still with us in the shape of the changed Church that its teachings led to. How we understand the role of the bishops in the Church, relative to one another, to the bishop of Rome, and to the people they serve, was given new clarity in the document. So too, *Lumen Gentium* changed how we think about the roles of the laity in the Church and how we think about holiness relative to all sections of the Church. It led directly to a renewed sense of the importance of baptism and it introduced the important idea of the pilgrim Church. Most of all, however, it is still with us in the particular struggles and challenges of our present moment in the history of the Church. It is this presence that will occupy us in this book.[1]

---

[1] I take the title of this book from the appeal of Bishop Wilhelmus Bekkers of the Dutch Diocese of 's-Hertogenbusch during the third session of the Council in 1964

The phrase "unfinished business," which I will use frequently in this book, refers to the complex relationship between *Lumen Gentium* and the tensions in today's Church. The clearest way in which *Lumen Gentium* remains a living presence in our Church is its implication in the various ecclesial challenges of our day. *Lumen Gentium* was not always clear and certainly did not always dot every *i* and cross every *t*. The ambiguities and the occasional lack of clarity in the text connect directly to many questions in today's Church: the authority of bishops relative to the role of the laity, the degree to which Church authority should or should not be as centralized in Rome as is currently the case, the nuances of an ecclesiology of the People of God and an ecclesiology of communion, and the relationship between the Church and the other great world religions. These and other issues are in play in the tensions in Roman Catholicism today, and it is the relationship between these concerns and the text of *Lumen Gentium* that we will explore in the pages that follow. It is my conviction that much of the malaise of Roman Catholicism today is to be attributed to ambiguities and lack of clarity in the texts of the Council documents in general and in *Lumen Gentium* in particular.

In consequence, this recognition of *Lumen Gentium* is at least as much about the present-day Church[2] as it is about Vatican II, and the structure of the book will confirm it. Each of the three parts takes up a major theme of the Constitution, first analyzing the text and identifying some of the questions with which it leaves us. The first three chapters of the book look closely at how *Lumen Gentium* treats the role of the bishop in the Church and relates the less-than-entirely satisfactory presentation to various tensions in today's Church between the global and the local levels. In the second part of the book it will be the turn of the laity, in particular the mixed blessing of describing them in the category of "secularity." How has this helped or hindered the evident emergence of the laity from the condition of passivity, if not infantilization, to which they had become inured through many previous centuries? Part 3 will focus more closely on

---

for ongoing commitment to religious freedom, ecumenism, and freedom within the Church, as well as Curial reform and an episcopal senate. Quoted in Xavier Rynne, *Vatican Council II* (Maryknoll, NY: Orbis, 1999), 290.

[2] Throughout this text, unless otherwise noted, the word "Church" or the phrase "Catholic Church" should be understood to refer to the Roman Catholic Church and to those other Churches in communion with the bishop of Rome.

the passages in *Lumen Gentium* where the Council fathers explore the relationships between the Church and the People of God and, indeed, the ways in which all people are offered salvation. This will lead to a sketch of an ecclesiology of humility as a way of linking the vision of *Lumen Gentium* and the needs of today's world where the presence and significance of the Church must be understood differently from the way in which it was in even the relatively recent past. If it is true to say, as *Lumen Gentium* does, that all people are somehow related to the People of God and true too that a measure of God's grace is to be found throughout the world and even among those who either do not know Christ or do not choose to follow him, the Church must find a humbler way to be present.[3]

I would like to thank a number of individuals for the help and inspiration they have given me in the present task. My colleagues in the religious studies department at Fairfield University continue to provide the supportive and collegial academic community that makes all our work easier. Among them I have, as always, to single out John Thiel, without whose keen editorial eye over the years I would have been guilty of many infelicities of expression. His invitation to deliver a plenary address at the 2011 annual meeting of the Catholic Theological Society of America was the instigation of much that is to be found in the third and final part of this book. My department chair Nancy Dallavalle, who works closely with me in the field of Catholic studies, has also been very helpful—more, I am sure, than she realizes. And I must thank in a special way Michael Fahey, SJ, currently scholar-in-residence at Fairfield University, who has carefully read my manuscript and given me the benefit of his enormous erudition with unstinting generosity. Further afield, the members of the New York area theological reading group that spun off from the Nashville-based Workgroup for Constructive Theology have been a remarkable and congenial collection of friends and scholars who model the best kind of academic companionship: Teresa Delgado, Jeannine Hill Fletcher, Elena Procario Foley, Roger Haight, SJ, Brad Hinze, Michele Saracino, and John Thiel. I am also grateful to the leadership of the Catholic Theological Association of Great Britain who invited me to give the plenary address on *Lumen Gentium* that

[3] Portions of this text have been previously published elsewhere, and I am grateful for the approval of their reprinting here from the editors of *Concilium, Horizons, New Blackfriars,* and the *Proceedings of the Catholic Theological Society of America.*

led me to start thinking about a council as an open-ended event, even as "a council that will never end." Obviously, none of these people can be blamed for the conclusions I have come to or the errors I have stubbornly insisted on retaining.

In addition, I would like to thank Hans Christoffersen of Liturgical Press, for his encouragement with the project and light hand on the tiller; the staff of Fairfield University's Center for Catholic Studies and Center for Faith and Public Life, for providing a wonderfully congenial day-to-day working environment; and my students at Fairfield University and Yale Divinity School, for making me think and speak more clearly than I would otherwise be inclined to do. I also want to offer a special word of thanks to a group of people who have no collective name but who, for the past eight years, have been showing up at Fairfield University three times a semester for two-hour workshops on Saturday mornings, to study many facets of the Catholic Church. I could call them "the Living Theology crowd." You know who you are, and you should know that you are an inspiration to me. And then, of course, there is my administrative coordinator Elyse Raby, who makes it easy to come to work every day and whose interest in and insightful observations about this present work have undoubtedly made it a better book though not as good, I would venture, as the one she will one day write herself.

And finally, as always, my wife and son. Jonathan now cheers me on from a little farther afield where he is pursuing his own career in music but remains genuinely supportive. And my spouse, life partner, and best friend Beth Palmer continues to inspire me with her dedication to her musical craft, her discipline, and her perfectionism. And she reminds me almost daily that any rumors of my impending canonization are grossly exaggerated. This is truly a blessing.

Introduction

The Unfinished Business
of *Lumen Gentium*

M ost commentators on the Second Vatican Council would
agree that the Dogmatic Constitution on the Church,
Lumen Gentium, is the single most important document
of the sixteen that the Council ratified.[4] Whether or not one concurs,
there is no question that the central concern of Vatican II was the
Church and that *Lumen Gentium* is the document that reflects most
directly upon the nature of the Church. Consequently, it is not difficult to sustain the claim that the most authoritative teaching on
the Church in recent centuries is to be found in this text, that it has
not been superseded, and that indeed it continues to be the basis
for current thinking about the nature and purpose of the Church.
One can certainly argue about this or that point of interpretation,
and there are some who believe that the document as a whole is
misrepresented and misunderstood. But no one who is actually in
communion with the Roman Catholic Church can make the case that
Lumen Gentium is anything other than of fundamental significance.

This book is written to celebrate the fiftieth anniversary of the
ratification of *Lumen Gentium* and takes very seriously the document's
centrality to Vatican II, and through Vatican II to the contemporary

[4] A word about the translation of the Council documents employed throughout
this book. I have selected the edition *Vatican Council II: The Basic Sixteen Documents*,
prepared by Austin Flannery, OP, which employs inclusive language wherever possible (Northport, NY: Costello, 1996). This very readable text is admirable in its
intentions and insufficiently familiar to the public.

Catholic Church. But a document of a general council of the Church is not Sacred Scripture. It is a historical document, which means that it needs to be understood in its historical context, and, while it is enormously authoritative, it is not the last word on anything. It stands as an important monument within a tradition that takes tradition very seriously, as one important text in an ongoing story of change. All discussion of *Lumen Gentium* has to begin from the text and to grant it the authority it possesses, but like any other text it is subject to imprecision and incompleteness. Incompleteness is an inescapable facet of history, a recognition that no text ever says the last word, just as the only historical phenomenon not open to change is something that is already dead. That being said, the only movement of a document with the authority that this one possesses is movement forward. *Lumen Gentium* cannot be gainsaid or amended, still less placed aside in favor of the way things used to be. But it can be built upon and even surpassed as its insights are reread in an age that it did not anticipate. The truths on which it builds may be eternal, but the words it uses are inevitably provisional. There are some, and I count myself among them, who believe that the lessons of Vatican II have not yet been entirely absorbed by the Church, and there are certainly others who think that the Council's teachings have been distorted in one way or another. But there is a further interpretive possibility.

If the provisionality of the text is a characteristic of any and every historical document, there are particular reasons to explore the elements of imprecision in *Lumen Gentium* and consequently to raise the question of what unfinished business the document has left to the Church. Principal among these is the well-known clash of perspectives among the Council fathers over the nature of the Church and thus about the kinds of teaching that a document on the Church ought to include. As we shall see below, one of the ways in which these potentially damaging differences can be finessed is to allow for the inclusion in the text of somewhat different articulations of the same eternal truths, so that each interest group can find enough of its own perspective in the text that it is satisfied and votes to approve. With the passage of time, however, a consequence of this practice is that reading the documents comes to be either a battleground on which differing interpretations are in conflict with one another or an effort to explain away the perspective with which one does not agree. To some extent, therefore, the tactic that was necessary to obtain the overwhelmingly positive votes on the Council documents in general, and *Lumen Gentium* in particular, is today being paid for by confusion about what the Council meant. Solving a short-term problem may have come back to haunt the Church of today.

As we proceed through this discussion of the unfinished business of *Lumen Gentium*, we will see that so many of our current ecclesial tensions and concerns can be traced back to lack of clarity or lack of completeness in the text of the Constitution. Some of this could have been anticipated and avoided, some of it is just the way history works. But all of it has left today's Church with the unfinished business that surrounds us. So what does it mean to talk about the "unfinished business" of *Lumen Gentium*? This is an important question for a number of reasons, not least because it sidesteps the long and increasingly sterile standoff between the proponents of a "hermeneutic of continuity" and "a hermeneutic of reform." It does not matter whether we focus, along with the more conservative interpreters who form the "continuity" group, on the texts themselves, or whether, with the progressives, we prefer to hone in on the rhetorical standpoint or the "event-character" of the Council. In either case it is quite possible to consider the work of the Council in general and *Lumen Gentium* in particular to be unfinished.

For the strict constructionists who wish to stress only the text of the sixteen documents of Vatican II and to ignore the Council "as event," the documents are still full of unfinished business. As we shall see, in *Lumen Gentium* itself there are many *lacunae* and indeed it exhibits a measure of internal conflict or even contradiction. It would be a mistake to think that because we are committed as interpreters to the text and the text alone, this in itself is unproblematic. Just as there is a conflict of interpretations between those who stress the text and those who stress the event, so there is also room for serious conflict of interpretation within the text of the conciliar constitution itself. Any notion that the overwhelming margin by which *Lumen Gentium* was ratified means that the over 95 percent who approved it had no misgivings about any of it would be greatly mistaken. Liberals and conservatives alike agonized before they recorded their *placet*, and in a number of places in the document the reader can see genuinely different ecclesiologies at work, side by side. It was almost as if the Council fathers voted to put the larger problem of interpretation of their words in the hands of the future. Perhaps they did all they could do and, conservatives and progressives alike, left a greater clarity in the lap of the Holy Spirit.

xvi   *A Council That Will Never End*

Those who believe the key to the importance of the Council is not found solely in the documents but equally, if not more so, in the Council's impact on the Catholic Church will see "unfinished business" somewhat differently. For them, it may depend on what we think *Lumen Gentium* set out to do, what the Council (of which it was the lynchpin) truly meant, and what the story of the Catholic Church in recent times has been, into which this episode and this document fits. In other words, for these people, approaching the unfinished business must wait until determining the genre of the document and the story of the Council. In *Vatican II: Did Anything Happen?* Joseph Komonchak examines Vatican II as an "event" and makes the point among many others that "an event has meaning only within a series," and the series is indefinite.[5] In other words, the meaning of the Council as a whole or any one of its documents is a product of its place in a sequence of events. But who is to determine when the sequence begins or ends (because upon that decision rests the kind of story in which it has its place, and hence its meaning)? Moreover, as time moves on and the series within which the event has its place grows larger and longer, the significance of the event may change quite dramatically. So much of today's intraecclesial wrangling about the meaning of the Council has only been made possible by the passage of time. And if *Lumen Gentium* introduced a measure of change into ecclesiology—a fact even those committed to the principle of continuity would have to admit—the document itself is neither the source of change nor the end of change, so much as it is historical testimony to the dynamism of the Church.

While these are interesting and important questions that we will return to in the body of the book, here in the introduction we are going to explore the question of unfinished business in a slightly different way. To aid us in this task we will take advantage of a fortunate historical coincidence. If Pius X had been a little more Herod-like and if he had had his own magi to forewarn him, there might have been a second massacre of the innocents in 1904. It was not a good year for theologians, but it was a positively outstanding year for newborns destined to be great theologians, babies who would celebrate their sixtieth birthdays the year that the Council fathers at

---

[5] Joseph Komonchak, "Vatican II as an Event," in *Vatican II: Did Anything Happen?* ed. David G. Schultenover (London and New York: Continuum, 2007), 24–57.

Vatican II finally ratified *Lumen Gentium*. Just imagine the heartache that Cardinal Alfredo Ottaviani might have been saved if there had never been a Bernard Lonergan, a Karl Rahner, an Yves Congar, and a John Courtney Murray! No method in theology, no horizon of mystery, no lay people in the Church, and no freedom of religion. Transcendental Thomism would have fizzled out, *la nouvelle théologie* would never have needed naming, and the Council fathers would have been without one particular American Jesuit to help them come to terms with modernity. Indeed, it is possible that there might have been no Council at all and *Humani Generis*[6] might have been the last word. Or perhaps it would have been the one-session council that the curial party's damage-control apparatus fervently desired. There are certainly other major theologians who might have carried the torch in the absence of these four, but one cannot deny that the face of twentieth-century Catholic theology would have been quite different without them. So let us use this conceit to structure the remainder of this introduction and call upon those four babies from 1904, Bernard Lonergan and Karl Rahner, John Courtney Murray and Yves Congar, to help us think our way through the unfinished business of *Lumen Gentium*, though not, of course, to its completion. Unfinished business is ever-present in a Church committed to a living tradition.

Theology in Its New Context

"Theology has become an empirical science in the sense that Scripture and Tradition now supply not premises, but data."

—*Bernard Lonergan*[7]

It is commonplace of commentary on the Council documents to reflect that they are masterpieces of compromise. Because they were the work of so many who inevitably had different views on this, that, or the other thing, and because they were written to produce overwhelmingly favorable vote counts, they seem often to be taking back with the left hand what they have so generously given with

---

[6] Encyclical of Pius XII in 1950, which condemned much of the work of *la nouvelle théologie*, the group of mostly French and Belgian theologians, including Congar, Jean Daniélou, Marie-Dominique Chenu, and Henri de Lubac.

[7] Bernard Lonergan, *A Second Collection* (Philadelphia: Westminster, 1974), 58.

the right. *Lumen Gentium* provides examples of just such a disposition, none better than what we find in the order of chapters in the text. Of course, as is well-known, the original order of themes in the early drafts of the document gave way to something quite different, especially in the decision to treat the whole "People of God" before the various divisions within the Church, in line with *Lumen Gentium*'s fresh emphasis on the importance of baptism. Similarly, the placing of the chapter on the universal call to holiness before that of religious life addresses the longstanding implication that somehow the life of the evangelical counsels is a higher calling than that of Christians living in the secular world. But what are we to make of placing the chapter on the hierarchical character of the Church before that on the laity, and how should we assess the significance of the first sentence of the chapter on the laity, clearly placing them outside "the hierarchy"?[8] What, in other words, is the balance—if indeed one can be found—between a vision of the Church as "the whole People of God" and one of it as a community clearly divided into those who are the hierarchy and those, the laity, who are clearly not?

Lonergan's work helps us to make sense of the two competing theologies that are evidently present in *Lumen Gentium*. Lonergan identifies the earlier form of theology as one that came into existence at the time of the Enlightenment. This "dogmatic theology" emerged in opposition to the scholastic theology it supplanted and "it replaced the inquiry of the *quaestio* by the pedagogy of the thesis. It demoted the quest of faith for understanding to a desirable, but secondary and, indeed, optional goal. It gave basic and central significance to the certitudes of faith, their presuppositions and their consequences."[9] In the twentieth century and especially at Vatican II, a new form of theology, similar to the old in that it is "locked in an encounter with its age," emerged. The new theology is empirical rather than deductive, local and particular and evolving rather than adhering to classicist values of universality and permanence, and accompanied by a new vocabulary and imagery. The Aristotelian conceptual apparatus has gone out of fashion and very quickly "the vacuum is being filled with biblical words and images, and with ideas worked out by historicist, personalist, phenomenological, and

---

[8] "Having described the functions of the hierarchy, the holy council is pleased to turn its attention to the state of those Christians who are called the laity" (LG 30).

[9] Lonergan, *A Second Collection*, 57.

existential reflection."[10] Most important in what Lonergan identifies as the empirical approach is the recognition of historicity. The earlier dogmatic theology talks of human nature and analyses the human person in terms of soul and body. The new theology "adds the richer and more concrete apprehension of man as incarnate subject."[11]

What if we employ Lonergan's notion of the human person as "incarnate subject" in a critical analysis of the idea of the Church in *Lumen Gentium*? Will it perhaps help us to begin to see some of the unfinished business? Just as when we look at the human subject in the drama of history we find ourselves face-to-face with the question of meaning, so when we see the Church as a kind of collective incarnate subject in history, we are similarly open to the play of historical forces. In our age, says Lonergan, we have come to see that the human subject is formed by acts of meaning, that they proceed from free and responsible persons, that meanings differ from culture to culture and nation to nation, and that in the course of time they change and they may go astray. Just so, the Church is not a given, preserved from historical vicissitudes. Because the Church is surely to be seen by Christians as vital to the implementation of God's salvific will, it does not follow that its passage through history is planned out by God. There is divine oversight from all eternity, but a design is not a plan. God is not a planner.[12] The Church is constituted anew by multiple human choices and actions, beset by national and cultural differentiation, open to change and even to decay.

The unfinished business of *Lumen Gentium* to which Lonergan leads us to attend is not, then, the struggle between the classicist and the more modern approach to the meaning of Church, so much as the historicity of *Lumen Gentium* itself. *Lumen Gentium* as an event in a story is not about the triumph, temporary or permanent, of a liberal, mid-twentieth-century vision of Church over the post-Tridentine, neo-Scholastic model. Rather, *Lumen Gentium* is the demonstration of the never-ending story of historical accident. The unfinished business of *Lumen Gentium* to which Lonergan alerts us is that of its own

[10] Ibid., 60.

[11] Ibid., 61.

[12] Planning is a temporal activity, and God the Creator does not plan history, or there would be no human freedom. God's design allows for human planning, of course, but planning—like any activity in history, even that of God within history—is contingent, accidental, and open to failure.

contingent and nonprogrammatic character. The importance of *Lumen Gentium* lies neither in the proclamation of theological novelty nor in the reiteration of timeless truths, but in its facticity as testimony to historical change. Change, not progress. The unfinished business of *Lumen Gentium* is a clearer understanding of how theological business is, of its nature, unfinished. What it leaves unclear is its own provisionality, and here there is something of a self-contradictory quality, for we can easily slip into thinking of the significant reforms promoted in the Constitution, like the place of the laity in the Church, the understanding of episcopal collegiality, and the focus on baptism and mission as so self-evidently superior to what they replace that they can be embraced as, finally, timeless truths for our time. But *Lumen Gentium* is "locked in an encounter with its age," time-constrained and historically conditioned in its conclusions, but programmatic in its demonstration that theology isn't just a product of the theological tradition, "but also of the cultural ideals and norms that set its problems and direct its solutions."[13]

Lonergan cannot, of course, leave the new theological historicism without some kind of foundation, located in a method found not in prescriptions but in "the grounds that govern the prescribing." The scientific analogy to what he is seeking in the religious realm would be something similar to Thomas Kuhn's "paradigm shift,"[14] that fundamental change to a new model of understanding that seems to come out of nowhere, though hindsight will reveal it as the mysterious result of painstaking research, and which legitimates itself in the spur it gives to further creativity. In religion, as is well-known, Lonergan identifies this as the moment of *conversion*, which "is not merely a change or even a development; rather, it is a radical transformation on which follows, on all levels of living, an interlocked series of changes and developments."[15] This conversion occurs in the incarnate subject, but it can surely also be an aspect of the Church as a collective incarnate subject. The Council's awareness of the importance of history is nicely captured in its own phrase, "reading the signs of the times," a phrase found in *Gaudium et Spes*

---

[13] Lonergan, *A Second Collection*, 58.
[14] Thomas Kuhn, *The Structure of Scientific Revolutions* (Chicago: Chicago Press, 1962).
[15] Lonergan, *A Second Collection*, 65–66.

(4), and not in *Lumen Gentium*.[16] But there is a connection between the two: *Gaudium et Spes* enunciating the norms and strategies for engagement with the world, *Lumen Gentium* having provided the account of ecclesial conversion.

A further aspect of the unfinished business of *Lumen Gentium* is thus revealed to be the need to see it as an act of ecclesial *metanoia* or change of heart. The change of heart, however, is not to a liberal perspective rather than a conservative one; instead, it is to the historicist recognition that the meaning of the Church is negotiated anew in each age, in an encounter with the age. Hence the significance of the shift from the static notion of a "perfect society" to the dynamism of the historical people of God. This ecclesiological insight makes attention to the age normative but does not make the insights generated in a particular age normative. So what is normative, in the words of Gianni Vattimo, is a kind of "formal commandment," the commandment to love, which looks to applications "that must be invented in dialogue with specific situations and in light of what the Holy Scriptures have revealed."[17] What caused the demise of the classical model were not its particular judgments, some of which were and remain valuable, but its denial of history. In tying itself to a particular age it tied the hands of the Gospel and denied its "productive noncontemporaneity," to use Johann Metz's ugly but insightful phrase.[18]

The Coming of the World Church

One of the biggest interpretive puzzles of *Lumen Gentium* is the question of how it understands the relationship between the Church and other Christians and between Christians and the other great world religions. The puzzle, indeed, is largely of its own making, for there are a number of statements that are quite hard to reconcile.

---

[16] A second essay in the Schultenover collection (see n. 2 above) brilliantly analyzes the Council as an event of twentieth-century history. In the midst of continuing difference and disagreement, symbolized in the more or less exact coincidence of the opening of the Council and the Cuban missile crisis, *Lumen Gentium* sees the Church as a sign and focus of unity. See Stephen Schloesser, "Against Forgetting: Memory, History, Vatican II" in O'Malley, *Vatican II: Did Anything Happen?* 92–152.

[17] Gianni Vattimo, *Belief* (Stanford, CA: Stanford University Press, 1999), 66.

[18] Johann Baptist Metz, "Productive Noncontemporaneity" in Jürgen Habermas, ed., *Observations on the Spiritual Situation of the Age: Contemporary German Perspectives* (Cambridge, MA: MIT, 1985), 169–80.

There is the notoriously ambiguous claim that the one Church of Christ *subsists in* the Roman Catholic Church (LG 8), which is read by some as a generous openness to the saving significance of Christian denominations beyond the Catholic tradition, while for others it apparently makes clear that it is the Church of Rome alone that possesses the message of salvation in its fullness. In the end the two sides here more or less agree on the facts, but the fear factor leads them to differ on whether the ecumenical cup is half full or half empty. Of more significance might be the challenge of reconciling the bald statement that "this pilgrim church is required for salvation" (LG 14), with the evident commitment to the notion of the universal availability of salvation to be found in the following words:

> Nor will divine providence deny the assistance necessary for salvation to those who, without any fault of theirs, have not yet arrived at an explicit knowledge of God, and who, not without grace, strive to lead a good life. Whatever of good or truth is found amongst them is considered by the church to be a preparation for the Gospel and given by him who enlightens all men and women that they may at length have life. (LG 16)

While this passage continues to insist that it is through Christ that all are saved, nevertheless it imagines divine grace reaching non-Christians through their own religious traditions, and unbelievers through their human goodness.

This picture of the universal will to salvation in *Lumen Gentium* is rightly associated with the influence of Karl Rahner, but not in an uncomplicated way. For Rahner, as usually represented, the fact of God's universal salvific will revealed in Holy Scripture and the fact that most human beings in history have not known the Christian God leads to the inescapable conclusion that this majority are saved in Christ, but through their own traditions. While this in itself is a challenging claim on a number of fronts, it becomes more interesting when we place it alongside Rahner's well-known utterance that in the Second Vatican Council we see "the coming of the world church."[19] The clear proclamation of a belief in the universal avail-

---

[19] Karl Rahner, SJ, "Towards a Fundamental Theological Interpretation of Vatican II" in *Vatican II: The Unfinished Agenda*, ed. Lucien Richard, Daniel Harrington, and John W. O'Malley (New York: Paulist, 1987), 9–21. This collection of essays was published to commemorate the twenty-fifth anniversary of the Council.

ability of salvation, if Rahner is correct, coincides with the end of
European cultural hegemony in the Catholic Church, or at least with
the beginning of the end. Rahner recognized its tentative nature and
was suitably prescient about Roman efforts to stem the devolution-
ary tide. Nevertheless, he appears to offer a stronger reading of the
words of *Lumen Gentium* quoted above when he says that they imply
"the possibility of a properly salvific revelation-faith even beyond
the Christian revelatory word."[20] Perhaps Rahner let his famous
guard down a little here, implying, it would seem, that not all of
God's grace is mediated through Christ. In fact, if he were alive and
saying something like this today, he might be called upon to explain
himself and could well fall under the same kind of Vatican suspicions
that have bedeviled more than a few of his Jesuit brothers in the
last thirty years.

Lumen Gentium is ambiguous about the role of the Catholic Church
relative to God's will to the salvation of all. But the very ambiguity
is the point. Indeed, the famously overwhelming majorities with
which Council documents were approved might be a sign of the
Council fathers recognizing the ongoing and unfinished nature of
the debates, just as much as, if not more than, the usual explanation that the documents were so equivocal that there was something
for everyone to vote for. It is hard to read *Lumen Gentium* and not
see a clear reiteration of the doctrine that the one Church of Christ
subsists in the Catholic Church. But it is also hard to read it and not
see glimmers of "the possibility of a properly salvific revelation-faith
even beyond the Christian revelatory word," as suggested by Rahner.
It is also quite hard to see how the two can be smoothly reconciled.

If one of the characteristics of *Lumen Gentium* is its open-endedness
on a whole variety of issues, whether we like this measure of ambiguity or not, its treatment of the universal availability of divine grace is
crystal clear. The debates at the Council and in subsequent decades
do not put the fact into question, only the matter of its relationship
to the Church as the sacrament of salvation. *Lumen Gentium* as an act
of the Council is also an act of the emergent world Church. Rahner
makes this point very clearly, arguing that even though the document tends to be answering European problems in a European way,
nevertheless it does "proclaim a universal and effective salvific will of

[20] Ibid., 14.

God which is limited only by the evil decision of human conscience and nothing else," and therefore that in comparison with previous theology in general and the neoscholastic mind-set of the original council schemata, "basic presuppositions for the world mission of the world Church are fashioned which were not previously available."[21]

With regard to the coming of the world Church and the operations of the "universal and effective salvific will of God," the unfinished business of *Lumen Gentium* is to keep the conversation going. The challenge to this task does not come from those who wish to assert the position maintained in *Dominus Iesus*,[22] where non-Catholic Christian communities are described as "defective," or at least not *because* they maintain that position, but from those who wish to foreclose the discussion and terminate the emergence of a truly world Church in which European intellectual or theological hegemony would not be taken for granted. The position of Benedict XVI was instructive in this regard. Problems arise not so much because of his commitment to *Dominus Iesus*, even with its ungenerous vocabulary of deficiency, but with his generally Eurocentric focus, as illustrated so clearly in the 2006 Regensburg address.[23] The red herring of pointless hurts to Muslim sensibilities aside, the general tenor of the address is a ringing endorsement of the heritage of Greek thought. When we peel away the layers of the inculturational onion of Christian doctrine, we will find at the heart, thought the pope, not the end of the onion but a kernel of Hellenist philosophy and theology. It is hard not to see this as an assertion that Athens—and hence the theology of the Roman Catholic Church—escapes the historical condition.

The Role of the Local Church

If we were to draw up a list of Vatican II teachings that seem, in the intervening years, to have been more honored in the breach than in the observance, that of the collegiality of the bishops would be

[21] Ibid., 13–14.

[22] "Declaration on the Unicity and Salvific Universality of Jesus Christ and the Church" (2000), http://www.vatican.va/roman_curia/congregations/cfaith/documents/rc_con_cfaith_doc_20000806_dominus-iesus_en.html.

[23] "Faith, Reason and the University: Memories and Reflections" (2006), http://www.vatican.va/holy_father/benedict_xvi/speeches/2006/september/documents/hf_ben-xvi_spe_20060912_university-regensburg_en.html.

very high on the list. From the notorious *nota praevia* or "explanatory note" attached to the text of *Lumen Gentium* at the express order of Paul VI, whether he intended to protect an overwhelming "yes" vote or to undercut the Council's teachings, to the evisceration of the Rome Synod of Bishops that Paul had at first seemed to favor, to John Paul II's clever but confusing distinction between "affective" and "effective" collegiality, all have subverted *Lumen Gentium*'s evident intention to put the bugbear of conciliarism to rest. *Lumen Gentium* attempted to finesse the delicate balance of papal and conciliar authority by expressing them as two manifestations of the guidance of the Holy Spirit. Together with the third way the Spirit guides the Church, the so-called *sensus fidei*, these three cannot legitimately be in competition with one another, for the Spirit cannot be at war with itself. Nor, as befits a Trinitarian analogue, is there any priority among the three, though difference is surely present. One might say they have different roles in the economy of the Church, but fundamentally they are nothing more than the one power of the Holy Spirit, watching over God's Church.

As time has elapsed since the Council's work, it has become more and more apparent that the discussion of collegiality is an instance of a more fundamental concern—that of the balance between the local and the universal Church. One would have thought that the Council fathers' resounding opinion that a bishop becomes bishop in virtue of his ordination and not by some papal act of delegation would have set this issue to rest, not to mention *Lumen Gentium*'s firm insistence that the local church possesses all the elements of the whole church and is not a branch office of some ecclesiastical transnational. That this is not the case has been apparent in the extraordinarily frank exchanges that took place over a number of years between Cardinal Walter Kasper, champion of the priority of the local church, and the then-Cardinal Joseph Ratzinger, patron of the priority of the universal church.[24] The open-ended nature of

---

[24] Kasper took on Ratzinger initially in a book chapter, "Zur Theologie und Praxis des bischöflichen Amtes," in *Auf neue Art Kirche Sein: Wirklichkeiten—Herausforderungen—Wandlungen* (Munich: Bernward bei Don Bosco, 1999), 32–48. Ratzinger responded in an article in the *Frankfurter Allgemeine Zeitung* (December 22, 2000), 46. Kasper argued further in "On the Church: A Friendly Response to Cardinal Ratzinger," *America* 184 (April 21–30, 2001), and was answered yet again by Cardinal Ratzinger in *America* 185 (November 19, 2001). The easiest approach to this

this particular debate, though it ceased when Cardinal Ratzinger became pope, is in itself a part of the ongoing unfinished business of *Lumen Gentium*. Extreme conciliarism and extreme papalism both attempt to foreclose debate and fail to recognize the delicate balance that the Dogmatic Constitution sought to express. Indeed, the decline in the fortunes of collegiality and of the legitimate autonomy of the local Church in the last two or three decades is a product of efforts to frustrate the Council's intentions. *Lumen Gentium* did not seek, let us be clear, to overturn the papalism of Vatican I in favor of return to the Council of Constance,[25] but tried very hard to put both pope and Council in a suitably balanced relationship under the guidance of the Holy Spirit. The unfinished business of *Lumen Gentium* is to strive to keep the delicate balance alive.

Whether one is committed to the priority of the universal over the local church or the opposite, however, one can still value the special contributions of local churches, destined to become increasingly apparent to the degree that the Catholic Church is more and more a world church. Ironically enough, at Vatican II the local church whose culture had the most impact on the Council documents was the American Catholic Church, which is certainly not what comes to mind when we think of an emerging world church. Yet, it is hard not to see the significance of the American democratic experiment in the Council decree on religious freedom, and not easy to overestimate in particular the contribution of John Courtney Murray, SJ, to the sea-change that came about in the Catholic Church's understanding of its place in democratic societies. But when we explore in more detail, we discover that the insights of American democratic life actually return us to deep-seated Catholic roots. And nothing could provide us with a better example of the symbiotic relationship between the local and the universal church proclaimed in *Lumen Gentium* than Vatican II's

---

complicated set of exchanges is provided by an excellent overview from Kilian Mc-Donnell, "The Ratzinger/Kasper Debate: The Universal Church and Local Churches," *Theological Studies* 63 (2002): 227–50.

[25] In 1415 the Council issues its famous decree *Haec sancta synodus*, in which it asserted that "legitimately assembled in the holy Spirit, constituting a general council and representing the Catholic church militant, it has power immediately from Christ; and that everyone of whatever state or dignity, even papal, is bound to obey it in those matters which pertain to the faith, the eradication of the said schism and the general reform of the said church of God in head and members." See http://www .legionofmarytidewater.com/faith/ECUM16.HTM#4.

treatment of freedom of religion. The then-Cardinal Ratzinger was right to insist that the universal Church is not simply a federation of local churches. *Lumen Gentium* said as much. But Cardinal Kasper was equally correct to point out that there is no universal Church aside from or prior to the local churches of which it is composed. What neither of them seems to have considered, but which may be important to our consideration of unfinished business, is the extent to which local churches, reflecting their cultures, might take on somewhat different external forms from one another.

The genius of Murray's influence on *Dignitatis Humanae* is the way in which the document reflects the wisdom of American experience with religion and democracy, while formulating its discussion of religious freedom in terms not of rights or conscience but an application of natural law. Nineteenth-century continental European suspicion of the so-called Americanist heresy was fueled by the assumption that the disestablishment of religion entailed its restriction by and subordination to the power of the state.[26] In the United States, however, separation of powers was a mechanism developed to provide for the free exercise of religion and to keep religion in general and that of the majority in particular from undue influence in secular government. But Murray's influence on the Council fathers leads them beyond this kind of pragmatic argument to one in which the divine law requires individuals to seek truth, especially religious truth, but this search "must be carried out in a manner that is appropriate to the dignity and social nature of the human person: that is, by free enquiry" (DH 2).

It is a curiosity to which not enough attention has been devoted that Vatican II in general and *Lumen Gentium* in particular represent not so much a struggle between a premodern and a modern church as one between two distinguishable strands of modernism.[27] In *Lumen Gentium*'s openness to the future and in *Dignitatis Humanae*'s forceful advocacy for freedom of conscience in religion we can see Enlightenment values at work, values that, as Charles Taylor has pointed out, the Church needed to learn from modernity itself.[28] In the resistance

[26] Pope Leo XIII's apostolic letter to Cardinal James Gibbons on the Americanist heresy (1899) can be found at www.ewtn.com/library/PAPALDOC/L13TESTE.HTM.

[27] Joseph Komonchak is an exception in this regard. See Komonchak, "Modernity and the Construction of Roman Catholicism," *Cristianismo nella storia* 18 (1997): 353–85.

[28] *A Catholic Modernity: Charles Taylor's Marianist Award Lecture*, ed. James L. Heft (New York: Oxford, 1999), 13–37, esp. 16–18.

to these conciliar priorities we encounter another modernity, described by Komonchak as the effort to harness elements of modernity to create a "counter-modern church" whose authority "represents a classic illustration of that self-conscious, rationalized, and bureaucratized mode of thought in which Max Weber saw the distinctive mark of modernity."[29] Taylor, on his part, ascribes the resistance to the openness of modernity not to Christianity itself, but to "the project of Christendom: the attempt to marry the faith with a form of culture and a mode of society."[30] So, more important than the details of *Dignitatis Humanae* is the relationship established between the teaching of the universal Church and the culturally conditioned contribution of any local church, in this case that of the United States of America. Attention to the local church as a culturally distinct contributor to the reality of the universal church is a defense against a monolithic Christendom and a challenge to bureaucratized thinking.

Once again, we see that the unfinished business of *Lumen Gentium* is not to decide for the local church against the universal church but to maintain the two in right relationship to and in delicate balance with one another. The effort to foreclose the open-ended debate does not come from those who want to give some priority to the universal church, or at least not because they want to give such priority, but from those who cannot see the futility of the Christendom project. We should also remember that modernity itself, which so colors the liberal "wing" of the Council fathers, is not far from Christendom in its unthinkingly hegemonic assumptions about the perspectives of Western culture. Here, where modernity shades into postmodernity and the local and particular have voice over the universal, beyond metanarratives about the triumph of the West, of Christendom or of the Church, may be where we find the free space in which to continue the unfinished business of walking the tightrope between anarchic particularism and authoritarian universalism.

A Dance to the Music of Time

To think of Vatican II as an event in a series bounded by an eschatological horizon allows for the emergence of the genuinely novel without the expectation of progress toward an intrahistorical termi-

---

[29] Komonchak, "Modernity and the Construction of Roman Catholicism," 383.
[30] Ibid.

nus. The reign of God is all around us, within history, or constantly breaking into history, but not exactly being constructed as a historical phenomenon. The Church, an anticipation and a sign of the reign of God, can engage in reform or revolution and should perhaps do so from time to time, though not in order to make more progress. Change in the Church is not progress but rather renewal or, perhaps better, refreshment. Refreshment takes place, in Lonergan's term, when the Church is "locked in an encounter with its age," reading the signs of the times and striving to be for its own time that community within which the transcendent is celebrated and hoped for, in an eschatological rather than a historical horizon. Both *Lumen Gentium* and *Gaudium et Spes* see the Church in this way. We are a pilgrim people, says *Lumen Gentium*, but the pilgrimage we are on is directed to the reign of God, not to a historical utopia. We travel in hope and if we lose our way for a time it will not be because the map went missing but because we forgot the kind of journey we were on. Perhaps we thought there was just one way to go or some kind of shortcut to get "there," wherever "there" is. Christendom, neoscholasticism, a centralizing papacy—these are all so many misdirections for the pilgrim people not because they are conservative or "on the right" on some ideological spectrum, but because they have forgotten that eschatological hope, while it is within history, is not hope in any historical fix. The healthiest moments in Church history have been those where divine providence has not been mistaken for historical progress, indeed where we as a people have not been so sure where exactly we are "going," if we are "going" anywhere at all. To a degree, our postmodern world with its suspicion of universal reason and controlling metanarratives offers the Church a way beyond the instrumental rationality of modernity with which it has been infected. And when we look back with apparent nostalgia to the early Church, the Church of the first three centuries, it should not be because we think they had everything right or they were more liberal than we are or more conservative than we are. History makes evident that they had many challenges to their self-understanding and almost literally did not know where they were going. But lack of clarity meant only that everything except eschatological hope in the reign of the kingdom was in question. It is in this sense, quite unromantic, that the early age might be a model for us now.

The resources that *Lumen Gentium* employs for addressing the meaning of the Church are those of *aggiornamento* and *ressourcement*.

While *aggiornamento* is often translated as "bringing up to date," the connotations have more to do with a sense of renewal and refreshment than modernization, a term that inevitably implies the sense that we know better now. John XXIII's oft-quoted remark that he wanted to open the windows and "let in a little fresh air" exactly captures the sense of *aggiornamento*. And though *ressourcement* is rightly translated as "return to the sources," we are being invited to refresh ourselves in lively springs of water gushing out of the ground, not to bury ourselves in some moldy library basement filled with outdated answers to questions no longer asked. *Ressourcement*, for the most part, means to revisit the inspiration of the great fathers and mothers of the Church, all of them distinguished by a clear commitment to an encounter with their own age, whether it be an Origen or an Augustine or an Aquinas or a Teresa of Avila. In every case, *ressourcement* means reading them in their historical context for the wisdom they display in interpreting the Gospel for their times, not as systems for all time. They are, in Lonergan's felicitous phrase, "not premises, but data."[31]

There was no better twentieth-century exponent of the balance between *aggiornamento* and *ressourcement* than Congar, who championed the movement that came to be known as *la nouvelle théologie*, devoted as it was to the rehistoricizing of Christian tradition in the face of neoscholasticism and the aftermath of the modernist crisis. It was, indeed, the prominent neoscholastic Dominican theologian Reginald Garrigou-Lagrange who sarcastically labeled Congar, Marie-Dominique Chenu, and others as the "new theologians" and who aided Pius XII's attack on them in his 1950 encyclical *Humani Generis*. Garrigou-Lagrange's hatred for them, not too strong a word, was due as much to the plan of study of the Dominican *studium generale* Le Saulchoir, outlined by Chenu in a privately circulated manuscript in the late 1930s[32]—a text which led to his eventual removal from the

---

[31] A remarkable collection of essays on *ressourcement* can be found in a recent book not surprisingly titled *Ressourcement: A Movement for Renewal in Twentieth-Century Catholic Theology*, ed. Gabriel Flynn and Paul D. Murray (Oxford: Oxford University Press, 2012).

[32] It was Chenu in this text who really developed the idea of the importance of "reading the signs of the times," and it was Chenu who had the greatest influence on *Gaudium et spes*, a text declared too optimistic and to underplay "the cross" in favor of "the incarnation" by both Joseph Ratzinger and Karl Rahner. The text of *Le Saulchoir: Une ecole de théologie* is most easily obtainable as reprinted in a book by the

institution and long-term exile to Canada,[33] as it was to any work by Congar, Jean Daniélou, or Henri de Lubac, the other primary objects of his wrath. Chenu's schematic outline of the course of study at Le Saulchoir stressed reading tradition in a historically sensitive manner, an approach that raised once more the shibboleths of the modernist witch hunt.

While Chenu arguably had the greater influence on *Gaudium et Spes*, it was Congar whose thought ran through and through the text of *Lumen Gentium*. The stress on the central significance of the baptismal priesthood, the prominence of the role of the laity, the historical recall of episcopal collegiality, the location of ecclesiastical authority in the work of the Holy Spirit, all can be traced to Congar's ideas in his great work of the early 1950s, *Jalons pour une théologie du laïcat*.[34] He was by no means the only one—Gérard Philips was another[35]—but Congar's was the single biggest influence. However and somewhat ironically, the completion of *Lumen Gentium* coincided almost exactly with a radical revision in Congar's own ecclesiology.

Though there are a number of areas of unfinished business in *Lumen Gentium*, some of the more important of which we have touched on in this introduction, the way in which Congar addressed his own and *Lumen Gentium*'s treatment of the laity as "secular" is instructive for the way in which unfinished business needs to be conducted. In the original edition of *Lay People in the Church*, Congar had described the laity as those who do God's work in the world, those for whom "the substance of things in themselves is real and interesting," while the cleric is the one "for whom things are not really interesting *in themselves*, but for something other than themselves, namely, their

---

same name, which also includes interpretive essays by Giuseppe Alberigo, Etienne Fouilloux, Jean-Pierre Jossua, and Jean Ladrière, with a brief postscript by Chenu himself (Paris: Cerf, 1985).

[33] There is an amusing essay to be written on the various places of exile to which suspect French theologians were sent in the 1950s. Not for them any Devil's Island, unless the theological equivalent of such might be Canada (Chenu), Cambridge, England, and later Jerusalem (Congar) or, most improbable of all for a Frenchman, Daniélou's internal exile from the Jesuit house of studies at Fouvière near Lyons to Paris(!), where he became chaplain to a girls' lycée.

[34] Yves Congar, *Jalons pour une théologie du laïcat* (Paris: Cerf, 1953). *Lay People in the Church*, trans. Donald Attwater (Westminster, MD: Newman, 1957; original rev. 1964; rev. English, 1967).

[35] Gerard Philips, *The Role of the Laity in the Church* (Chicago: Fides, 1956).

relation to God."[36] In *Lumen Gentium* this becomes a reference to the "secular character," which is "proper and peculiar" to the laity, and "by reason of their special vocation it belongs to the laity to seek the kingdom of God by engaging in temporal affairs and directing them according to God's will" (LG 31). By this time Congar was revising his work to take account of criticism that he failed to break away from the clergy/laity division, and increasingly he began to write about "different ministries" rather than different classes of people. By the end of his life he could comment on the earlier Congar as someone who had fallen into the trap of defining the laity relative to the clergy and go on to make the quite different claim that "today it is the case, rather, that the clergy need to be defined in relation to the laity, who are quite simply members of the people of God animated by the Spirit."[37]

The example of an architect of *Lumen Gentium* having second and third thoughts about his own earlier ideas, ideas which influenced the Council document, brings us to a final dimension of the unfinished business, which is to be careful not to canonize the particular insights in the text. If *aggiornamento/ressourcement* is the theological method of refreshing the Church, it is the method rather than this or that particular judgment that needs to be the focus of unfinished business. Times change, and if theology is "locked in an encounter with its age," then theological insights important at one time may take a back seat at another.[38] Once again, looking at things this way puts into question the typical representation of the postconciliar era as a standoff between liberals and conservatives. While conservatives are undoubtedly at fault if they tie themselves to a historically conditioned theological system as if it were exempt from historicity, liberals can similarly be endangered by clinging to the insights of *Lumen Gentium* as if it were about to become the new dogmatics. *Lumen Gentium* is not "the truth." It is an effort to refresh the horizon of eschatological hope for a particular age. Fifty years on, its ideas have not been fully implemented in part because of ecclesiastical intransigence and in part because fifty years means that some of

[36] Congar, *Lay People in the Church* (1957), 17.

[37] The comments are recorded in *Fifty Years of Catholic Theology: Conversations with Yves Congar*, ed. and intro. Bernard Lauret (Philadelphia: Fortress, 1988), 65.

[38] On the volatility of theological truths, there is no better analysis than that to be found in John E. Thiel, *Senses of Tradition: Continuity and Development in Catholic Faith* (New York: Oxford, 2000).

the ideas are already dated. Times change, and the final unfinished business of *Lumen Gentium* may be to declare it both an historical document whose time is beginning to be past and a glorious effort to demonstrate the restoration of historical awareness in official theology. *Lumen Gentium* is "not premises but data," and its unfinished business is the recognition that its business—the business of theology—is and must be unfinished. The only final certitude is God's, and our access to it is not theology, but eschatological hope.

PART 1

The Ministry of Bishops

◻ ◻ ◻

He who searches hearts makes himself a beggar of love and questions us on the only really essential question, the premise and condition for pastoring his sheep, his lambs, his Church. Every ministry is based on this intimacy with the Lord; to live in him is the measure of our ecclesial service, which is expressed in an openness to obedience, to emptying of self . . . to total giving. Moreover, the consequence of loving the Lord is giving everything—absolutely everything, even one's very life—for Him: this is what must distinguish our pastoral ministry; it is the litmus test that shows how profoundly we have embraced the gift received in response to the call of Jesus and how we are joined to the people and the communities that have been entrusted to us. We are not expressions of a structure or an organizational need: even with the service of our authority we are called to be a sign of the presence and action of the Risen Lord, and so, to build up the community in fraternal charity.

—*Pope Francis's address to the Sixty-Fifth General Assembly of the Italian bishops, May 23, 2013*

Chapter 1

The Roles of Bishops in *Lumen Gentium*

Authority, the *Periti*, and the Faithful

L et us begin in what may seem a surprising place, thinking for a moment about the presence of the experts or *periti* who accompanied the Council fathers through the complex process of drafting and redrafting to which all the documents were somehow subject. There were several hundred of these men, some appointed by the pope, most brought along by a particular bishop as his trusted adviser.[1] It is difficult to overestimate their importance, especially in the innumerable seminars and conferences that they organized for the bishops in different language groups and their roles in aiding the bishops to draft their speeches and interventions in Council debates. It is also fascinating to see how the more conservative bishops like the immensely powerful Cardinal Alfredo Ottaviani tried so hard to exclude or limit the *periti*'s influence. Karl Rahner is reputed to have turned to Yves Congar and asked, "So, what are we here for?" when Ottaviani tried at the beginning of the first session to rule that the *periti* must be silent unless called upon to offer opinions. Of course the good cardinal's position on the Council can be measured by his well-known remark: "I hope I die before the end of the Council, because then at least I will have died a Catholic!"

It is important to begin with the *periti* and the role they played in the conciliar deliberations because it raises the question of how

[1] Anyone who would like to see how busy and how centrally engaged these theologians were need only browse in Yves Congar's fascinating *My Journal of the Council* (Collegeville, MN: Liturgical Press, 2012).

exactly the bishops understood what it meant to be teaching with authority. They evidently took their role with the utmost serious- ness, even to the point of asserting the infallibility of the collegial episcopate, and yet they equally knew that the final form of *Lumen Gentium* owed an enormous debt to a group of men who taught the teachers much that they otherwise would not have known. How can we make sense of this curious balance of responsibilities? There is certainly nothing said directly in the conciliar texts about the particular roles of theologians in the Church, though perhaps more is implied than was stated in comments such as the clear assertion that the laity "are called as living members to apply to the building up of the church and to its continual sanctification all the powers which they have received from the goodness of the Creator and from the grace of the Redeemer" (33). This does not exclude intellectual powers, and if it is true of the laity, then it is surely true of the clergy from among whom *all* the *periti* were chosen.

It seems safe to say that the episcopal authority the documents express is something in principle built upon the wisdom of the whole Church and not a fundamental or even preemptive step that delin- eates the boundaries within which all those not gifted with episcopal authority must thenceforward constrain their religious reflection. It is legitimate to draw such a conclusion either from statements like that in *Lumen Gentium* 33 above, which gives license to the natural gifts of all the baptized, or from the actual practice of the Council. In the latter case, the ways in which the bishops employed their *periti* show deference to those who may be more knowledgeable and a refreshing humility about the extent of their own gifts of theological reflection, without at all abandoning their responsibility as bishops to teach with the most solemn authority. This gift of teaching, even when employed infallibly, builds upon, subsumes, focuses, and gives expression to the faith of the whole Church. So the *sensus fidei*, which is the primary gift of the Holy Spirit to the whole community of faith, is a kind of backdrop or even prerequisite for the legitimate exercise of infallible conciliar or papal teaching—both of which are guaranteed by that same Spirit. If for no other reason, this explains why solemn papal teaching is intended to follow consultation with the entire Church. It may also help to explain how it is that for all their striking words the texts of the conciliar documents are not received with the shock that accompanies pure novelty but rather with an "Aha, so that's how it is."

This idea that authoritative teaching reflects and builds upon the *sensus fidei* is further supported by the well-known fact that the ordering of the chapters in *Lumen Gentium* itself makes an important ecclesiological statement. A lot of ink has been spilled on the decision to divide the original portion of the schema on the laity and to place half of it *before* the chapter on the hierarchical nature of the Church. Thus, chapter 2 became "the People of God," in which much is said about the fundamental equality of all the baptized and, indeed, of their priestly, prophetic, and "royal" status. It emphatically states that "the whole body of the faithful who have received an anointing which comes from the holy one cannot be mistaken in belief." This "supernatural sense of the faith [*sensus fidei*]" is visible in "a universal consensus in matters of faith and morals" (12). Only after this had been made clear did the Council turn to the discussion of the hierarchical nature of the Church, and then of the laity as a specific component of the faithful. First comes the affirmation of the unity and equality of the people of God; then follows differentiation into the various orders within the Church.

The way in which the term "the faithful" is treated in chapter 2 of *Lumen Gentium*, for all the excellence of the teaching, is another moment in which we encounter the kind of uncertainty or ambiguity that points to some of the unfinished business with which the document has left us. The problem may well stem from the important statement that "though they differ essentially and not only in degree, the common priesthood of the faithful and the ministerial or hierarchical priesthood are nonetheless interrelated; each in its own way shares in the one priesthood of Christ" (10). There are two significant consequences of this statement, neither of which is explicitly addressed in the document. The first is that because the two priesthoods differ "essentially," the one conferred in baptism and the second in holy orders, those who receive the sacrament of orders do not thereby lose their baptismal priesthood. They possess both. Herein lies the important insight that "the faithful" is an inclusive term and the ministerial priesthood is in this sense a subgroup of the faithful, not an order separate from them. The term "the faithful" is not a synonym for "the laity" but rather for "the People of God" as a whole. The second consequence follows on this; because the two priesthoods are "essentially" different one cannot say that the laity are somehow less priestly than the ordained, or that the ordained possess the fullness of a priesthood that is somehow less fully or perfectly held by the laity. Lay people, like the rest of the faithful, possess the fullness of baptismal priesthood. Whatever the priesthood of the ordained is, it is not more of the same. Purely in terms of priesthood, then, there is no justification for somehow ranking the ordained as above the laity. Their differentiation through the sacrament of orders places them alongside rather than above the laity, within the ranks of the baptismal priesthood. Their difference is that they are at the service of the whole, faithful in a way that the laity are not, though, as we shall see, the laity have their own proper function.

If we overlook the fact that an ordained minister is the possessor of both priesthoods and has not replaced the baptismal form with that of the hierarchical, it is easy to slip into thinking of the "faithful" as the unordained. On the whole, the document does not make that mistake, using phrases like "all the faithful, whatever their condition or state" (11) or pointing out that the Holy Spirit "distributes special graces among the faithful of every rank" (12). But here and there another more traditional perspective creeps in. For example, the pope is described as the "visible source and foundation of the unity both of the bishops and of the whole company of the faithful." Bishops are said to do their work by "arousing the fervent cooperation of the faithful" (23). Bishops are to be respected as teachers and "the faithful, for their part, should concur with their bishop's judgment" (25). Moreover, "the faithful . . . should be closely attached to the bishop" (27). Priests "should care for the faithful whom they have begotten spiritually" (28) and "the priesthood of Christ is shared in various ways both by the ministers and by the faithful" (62). While it may seem churlish to bring up these inconsistencies in a document that has made great strides forward in understanding the respective roles of the ordained and the laity, any teacher reading these missteps in a student's essay would recommend "another read-through" before final submission. Of course, given what we know about the dynamics of the conciliar debates it is hard to resist the conclusion that these less theologically happy distinctions were added to placate some bishops.

Thinking about the implications of the important role the *periti* played in the document and further dwelling on the significance of competing nuances in understanding exactly who "the faithful" are, we have encountered two significant pieces of unfinished business to do with the authority of the text. First, as we noted above, the authority of the conciliar voice is predicated upon the faith of the whole Church and comes to it as a confirmation of what it has always believed, not as some novel insight dropping from the skies. If this is correct, it has to mean that the forward movement of post-conciliar understanding will also involve further teaching that has taken serious account of the *sensus fidei* and that is not commonly expressed as a correction of what the Council understood to be the Spirit-inspired intuition of *all* the faithful. Second, even a supremely authoritative text like that of *Lumen Gentium* can be guilty of imprecision and consequently leave room for the important work of clarifying and, frankly, even amending the words on the page. And just as we saw that the assistance the *periti* furnished to the bishops did not undermine episcopal authority, so too we should recognize that conciliar documents, which are of their nature time-conditioned and may contain inaccuracies, are not thereby reduced in authority. The Holy Spirit at work in and through episcopal and even conciliar teaching is not magically producing perfection but "over the bent / World broods with warm breast and with ah! bright wings."[2]

Bishops at Vatican II: What Do They Say about Themselves?

With these two preliminary thoughts about the metaquestion of conciliar authority, we can now turn to the principal issue of this chapter: the conciliar treatment of bishops. In other words, we turn to what the bishops had to say about themselves. Immediately we face what can only be called a "high" interpretation of the role of the individual bishop in his diocese and of the bishops collectively or, as the Council prefers, collegially. Many authors have addressed this question of the elevated status of the bishop in conciliar teaching.[3] My concern is not to repeat their conclusions but to look into the texts in search of places where it leaves issues unclear and questions at least partially unanswered—that is, where there is unfinished business to which the Church of today needs to attend.

The bishops at Vatican II were at least to some degree concerned to right an imbalance in understanding episcopal authority created by

[2] Gerard Manley Hopkins, from "God's Grandeur."

[3] None better than Richard R. Gaillardetz in *The Church in the Making* (New York: Paulist, 2006), and in the more recent text jointly authored with Catherine E. Clifford, *Keys to the Council: Unlocking the Teaching of Vatican II* (Collegeville, MN: Liturgical Press, 2012), esp. 111–28.

the abrupt ending to the First Vatican Council. When the outbreak of the Franco-Prussian War so preoccupied the French that they could no longer protect the papacy, Rome became the final prize of Italian reunification and Vatican I could no longer continue. The Council ended before anything could be said about the role of the bishops that might have balanced the conciliar definition of papal infallibility. As a consequence, perhaps unintended, the years between the two Councils were marked by an excessive focus on the role of the pope at the expense of that of the bishops, either collectively or each in his diocese. For almost a century the pope ruled the Church through the Curia, and the Curia came to imagine not only that this was the best way to run the Church but, perhaps, that this was the way it had always been. As the assembled bishops began to think more closely about their collegial authority, they came into the head-on confrontation with the entrenched power of the Curia. Like much of the drama of the Council, this should not be interpreted as a stand-off between the good guys and the bad, still less between the conservatives and the liberals, but rather a genuine difference of ecclesiological opinion. However, like so many such disagreements, the waters are muddied when one "side" hews to a species of in-stitutional fundamentalism that the other counters by reference to theology and history. When the differences are represented by "no change" and "moderate change," the chances of reconciling the two positions are slim.

Once the conciliar majority had established their moderate reform-ist position, they addressed the set of issues surrounding the status of bishops in three ways: they clarified the basis for their episcopal authority, they engaged in a detailed theological reflection on the role of the bishop as head of the local church, and they affirmed the importance of the exercise of episcopal collegiality. First, episcopal authority is founded on apostolic succession, so that "the sacred synod consequently teaches that the bishops have by divine institu-tion taken the place of the apostles as pastors of the church" (20). "The fullness of the sacrament of Orders is conferred by episcopal consecration," as "through the imposition of hands and the words of consecration, the grace of the holy Spirit is given, and a sacred character is impressed." Moreover, "it is for bishops to admit newly elected members into the episcopal body by means of the sacrament of Orders" (21). Second, because they are "vicars and legates of Christ" the bishops "exercise a power which they possess in their own right and are most truly said to be at the head of the people whom they govern" (27). They are not delegates of the pope. Finally, "the collegiate character and structure of the episcopal order is clearly shown by the very ancient discipline whereby the bishops installed throughout the whole world lived in communion with one another and with the Roman Pontiff" (22). Always united with the bishop of Rome and never without him, the college of bishops "proclaim infallibly the doctrine of Christ" when—dispersed around the world or gathered in an ecumenical council—"they are in agreement that a particular teaching is to be held definitively" (25). Each of these three positions, however, is not without a measure of ambiguity.

One of the most important pieces of unfinished business with which *Lumen Gentium* has left us is that of adjudicating the relationship between change and continuity in ecclesiology. The two opening sections of chapter 3 of *Lumen Gentium* illustrate the "change versus no change" struggle in an exemplary way. Section 18, which opens the chapter on the hierarchical nature of the Church, begins by saying that "Christ the Lord set up in his church a variety of offices whose aim is the good of the whole body." Becoming more specific, the bishops declare that Jesus Christ "established the holy church by sending the apostles" and "willed that their successors, the bishops, should be the shepherds in his church until the end of the world." Having added a reference to the primacy of Peter, this section ends by declaring that "this teaching on the institution, the permanence, the nature and the force of the sacred primacy of the Roman Pontiff and his infallible teaching office" is proposed once again to be "firmly believed by all the faithful." In other words, the whole character of the twentieth-century Church, including the charism of papal infallibility, only dogmatically defined less than a hundred years previously, is located in the mind and will of the historical Jesus. There is no room for historical development in this version of the apostolic succession of the bishops.

Sections 19 and 20 tell the story in a narrative which recognizes the role of historical development. Whereas in the previous section, for example, Jesus is described as naming Peter as the head of the other apostles "in order that the episcopate . . . might be one and undivided," here Jesus places Peter at the head of the college of the apostles, with the intention that they will preach the Gospel to the ends of the earth, in the power of the Spirit that comes upon them at Pentecost. Moreover, the office of bishop is now reported not as something emerging from the will of Jesus Christ but as a decision of the apostles acting in faithfulness to the commission Christ had given them. "For that very reason," say the bishops, "the apostles were careful to appoint successors in this hierarchically constituted society" (20). This time the office of bishop is seen as a prudential historical decision of the apostles in order to ensure the future progress of the Church, not as an office already foreseen by Jesus in his establishment of the apostolic college. While it is surely the case that here we are informed that the office of bishop should be understood as a natural development of the early Church's concern for continuity, which they understood as the charge Jesus Christ had given to them, the prior section is not in agreement with this. Moreover, these two perspectives do not seem to be two competing accounts of the same historical development for, while sections 19–20 take the historical development of the early Church as given, and are consequently open to the fact of historicity, section 18 does no such thing. Instead, it begins from the facticity of the present-day Church and, no doubt, out of a faith-filled commitment to the ideality of today's Church, and sees no other way to anchor its permanence, and thus its escape from historicity, than to place it in all its details firmly in the mind of Christ. Clarity on this matter is evidently something with which *Lumen Gentium* did not provide us, though the faithful—all of the faithful—are surely entitled to one account that both confirms their faith in the Gospel and respects their intelligence as twenty-first-century human beings.

The declaration that it is the bishop who possesses the fullness of orders has complex implications and is also not without its challenges. Section 26 is a good place to start. The section begins with the parenthetic observation that the bishop is "invested with the fullness of the sacrament of Orders" and goes on to observe that the "church of Christ is really present in all legitimately organized local groups of the faithful," which, "under the sacred ministry of the bishop," is rightly seen as "a manifest symbol" of the unity of the community of faith (26). The bishops take leadership "personally in the name of Christ" and are not "to be regarded as vicars of the Roman Pontiff," since "they exercise a power which they possess in their own right and are most truly said to be at the head of the people whom they govern" (27).

Among the consequences and unfinished business of this understanding of the role of the bishop are the following: What is the relationship of the authority of the bishop to that of the pope? What are the implications for how we understand the role of the priest? If this picture of the bishop as the focus of unity of the local church is understood correctly, how many bishops should we have in the Church and what does it mean to be a titular bishop, whether an auxiliary in a diocese or a curial official in Rome?

Looked at historically there is no doubt that the bishop possesses the fullness of orders. In the ancient Church there was no Roman jurisdiction over other bishops; bishops were understood relative to the people in the local church to which they had been called. Bishops were selected in a variety of ways, some by acclamation and some through a selection process conducted by the bishops of the region. Each bishop, however selected, was then married to his diocese for the rest of his life. Over time, Rome came to exercise greater responsibility for confirming the jurisdiction of bishops and eventually for their selection and appointment to a particular diocese. Today, the ceremony of episcopal consecration does not proceed until a Roman "mandate" has been read aloud. But it has always remained the case that a bishop is consecrated by several of his fellow bishops, often from the area around the church over which he will preside and not by a single bishop. While there is a principal consecrator there must be at least two other bishops participating, and all bishops present share in the laying on of hands—the focal point of the ceremony. While the bishop's jurisdiction comes to him from Rome in recognition of his being in communion with the bishop of Rome, the fullness of orders he possesses is no less than that of the pope himself and is not derivative of papal authority. In his local church in communion with the Church of Rome, the bishop is the leader of a community that possesses all that is needed to be the Church.

While this high estimation of the role of the bishop is an important contribution to establishing a balance of authority between the local and universal Church, it is not without its problems. Principal among them is the enormous difference between the role of the bishop today and that of a bishop in the early centuries of the Church's life. Back then, the bishop was first and foremost the pastor of the local church, doing much the work of the pastor of one of today's parishes, though some bishops in certain churches—especially Rome—had influence beyond their own. Today the bishop is the administrator of a large and sometimes immense local church and through no fault of his own an unfamiliar person to most of those in his charge. Very few bishops in the American Church can exercise the direct pastoral responsibilities that present-day pastors do or that the bishops of the ancient Church were able to fulfill. Dioceses, even small ones, are too large. The need for help in accomplishing his ministry was the source and occasion of the office of presbyter and of deacon, understood as an assistant to the bishop, and this understanding of the priestly and diaconal roles is restored in *Lumen Gentium*. Auxiliary bishops are also commonplace in today's Church, and they exercise the sacramental roles of the bishop on his behalf, most notably the demands of confirmation ceremonies. But the administrative responsibilities of the bishop himself seem to have all but eclipsed his role as pastor and preacher.[4] Why is it that *Lumen Gentium* did not seem to recognize this problem, which has only grown worse in the intervening half century?

Assistant and coadjutor bishops are entirely absent from the text of *Lumen Gentium*. Priests are described as "assistants" in the work of the diocesan bishop. Indeed, titular bishops in general, which includes those who hold offices in the Vatican Curia, are not discussed in the text. This is remedied to a degree in the Decree Concerning the Pastoral Office of Bishops in the Church, *Christus Dominus*, but only by two brief sections (25–26) discussing the roles of auxiliary bishops and coadjutors. The auxiliaries are appointed only to help where a diocese is so large that a bishop cannot do all he is ordained to do; the coadjutors are bishops holding right of succession. But in neither case is there any discussion of their power of orders, and, in the case of both, there is no question of their holding jurisdiction. So, while the practice of dividing a huge diocese into smaller administrative units each led by an auxiliary bishop is not discussed here, nothing is to be done that would be problematic for "the unity of the diocesan administration and the authority of the diocesan bishop" (25).

From a purely practical point of view, the Church should obviously have many more bishops than it currently does if each is to be able to discharge the functions described in *Lumen Gentium*. Pragmatically, this implies the division of large dioceses into smaller units, each of which is presided over by a diocesan bishop. Perhaps this has not happened because there are administrative concerns that trump eccle-

---

[4] For a good discussion of these and associated problems, see Gaillardetz, *The Church in the Making*, 121–26.

siological considerations, though the documents of Vatican II neither say nor imply that such an order of priorities exists. Rather, they suggest that a diocesan bishop's role is, above all, pastoral and spiritual leadership, and that auxiliary bishops and priests aid him in his task. There is certainly nothing in *Lumen Gentium* or *Christus Dominus* to suggest that administrative convenience should override the apostolic role of the bishop. Pragmatic and ecclesiological reflection both seem to point toward decreasing the size of dioceses and consequently increasing the number of bishops, but this has not happened. There are doubtless a number of reasons why this path has not been followed, but one of them is surely that it is not imagined, still less promoted, in the Council document. If the absence of any consideration of this issue is not driven by administrative concerns—and if it were it would be quite uncharacteristic of the conciliar style—then it must surely be put down to a failure of the conciliar imagination. The way that the Church should be organized administratively should be a function of making it easier for bishops to fulfill their roles. But *Lumen Gentium* turns this around. The present size of most dioceses makes it nearly impossible for a bishop to be what the document itself says he should be, but no solution other than perhaps an increase in the number of auxiliary bishops seems to be envisaged. The Council left much unfinished business on the enormously important question of how the shape of the Church might be adjusted to make episcopal leadership more effective than it currently is.

The Code of Canon Law, whose purpose is to reflect the teaching of the Church in a juridical context, is not helpful in determining what exactly a bishop is. In fact, it further complicates an already unsatisfactory situation by describing bishops as of two kinds: diocesan and titular.[5] This clearly corresponds to the present-day reality, though certainly not the practice of the Church of the first few centuries, where the only bishop was one who presided over a local church. In the beginning a bishop without a diocese would have been inconceivable. Today it is a commonplace, though it is difficult to determine a theological rationale for understanding the episcopal role of someone who is either an assistant to the diocesan bishop or, even more curiously, a bishop without a diocese whose responsibilities in the Vatican Curia are almost entirely bureaucratic. Why the hierarchy

---

[5] Canon 376.

of priest, bishop, archbishop, and cardinal should be reflected in the career structure of the Curia is easy enough to explain historically but almost impossible to justify theologically. There is certainly both need and room to develop a theology of service that would enlighten the whole Church about the important role of the Curia, but such a theology need not and perhaps should not involve hierarchical ordering or episcopal status. There is absolutely no reason in principle why a suitably qualified lay person could not be the prefect of many of the congregations. Though it is a high office with significant responsibilities, it is bureaucratic rather than sacramental. The episcopal charism of governance relates only to diocesan bishops. However, one of the major factors that make it less likely that this avenue of ecclesial reform might be explored is the failure of *Lumen Gentium* to adequately consider the tension between the role of the bishops as administrator and as pastoral leader. There is unfinished business here.

The Vexed Question of Episcopal Collegiality

The discussions around the collegiality of the bishops were among the most contentious of all the conciliar debates, perhaps because the unstoppable force of the bishops' authority and the immovable object of papal primacy seemed to be on a collision course. The issue was at heart relatively simple; how could the teaching of Vatican I be completed or balanced without somehow undermining it? This at least was the anxiety of the more conservative of the Council fathers, and the long historical view of the Church typical of the Curia had to mean that some were worried about the specter of conciliarism—the debate about whether the authority of a Council was greater than that of the pope, sparked by the fifteenth-century Council of Constance.[6] The Council resolved or at least finessed this conflict by affirming the teaching authority of the body of bishops in the following words:

> The college or body of bishops has no authority, however, other than the authority which it is acknowledged to have in union

---

[6] See Brian Tierney, *Foundations of the Conciliar Theory: The Contribution of the Medieval Canonists from Gratian to the Great Schism* (Cambridge: Cambridge University Press, 2010), and Francis Oakley, *The Conciliarist Tradition: Constitutionalism in the Catholic Church, 1300–1870* (New York: Oxford University Press, 2008).

with the Roman Pontiff, Peter's successor, as its head, his primatial authority over everyone, pastors or faithful, remaining intact. For the Roman Pontiff, by reason of his office as Vicar of Christ and as pastor of the entire church, has full, supreme and universal power over the whole church, a power which he can always exercise freely. The order of bishops is the successor to the college of the apostles in their role as teachers and pastors, and in it the apostolic college is perpetuated. Together with its head, the Supreme Pontiff, and never apart from him, it is the subject of supreme and full authority over the universal church; but this power cannot be exercised without the consent of the Roman Pontiff. (22)

One would certainly think that this was sufficient protection for the authority of the pope, bought indeed at the price of considerable ambiguity about the collegial authority of the bishops. Just what are they doing when they teach in union with one another and with the bishop of Rome that in any way augments papal governance? They are certainly giving evidence of the unity in faith of the whole Church and its communion with the bishop of Rome, but if this is all that their collegiality consists in, why is it frequently cited as one of the great achievements of *Lumen Gentium* and why especially was even this too strong for the more conservative Council fathers, who pressured Paul VI to add an editorial comment, commonly known as the *nota praevia*, to the final text? The note contains a lot of technical distinctions, such as the clarification of the relationship between the ontological and juridical status of the bishop, but its real significance is in the overall toning down of the authority of the college of bishops and the strong restatement of the role of papal authority. Technically, the note is not part of the document but a clarification of the terminology used in it, but as John O'Malley has pointed out, whatever the intent "it gave those who opposed collegiality a tool they could—and would—use to interpret the chapter as a reaffirmation of the status quo."[7]

Our Church today shows evidence of the unfortunate consequences of ambiguity in the text of *Lumen Gentium*. We live with the continuing lack of clarity bequeathed to us by the Council. The exercise of papal authority under Paul VI and especially in the two

---

[7] John O'Malley, *What Happened at Vatican II* (Cambridge, MA: Harvard University Press / Belknap Press, 2010), 245.

pontificates of John Paul II and Benedict XVI seems to many to be a reversion to earlier patterns of papocentrism. Roman Catholic bishops are discussed in *Lumen Gentium* as the leaders of their local churches but frequently treated by the Roman Curia as if they are subordinates who work for the pope, if not for the Curia itself. Among the bishops themselves there are many who feel the constraints as irksome, and many who thrive within a more highly centralized church. When Bishop William Morris of Toowoomba in Australia fell under Vatican suspicion in 2010, it was the American Archbishop Charles Chaput who was sent to investigate and whose report, presumably, was instrumental in Bishop Morris being removed from office by Pope Benedict.[8] This is a report that Bishop Morris has yet to see. From Morris to Chaput, there is clearly much variation among the ways in which the balance of episcopal and papal authority is interpreted and very different levels of tolerance for the way it is exercised. That same room for different visions of authority was fostered by the ambiguity of *Lumen Gentium*, perhaps in order to obtain the overwhelming positive vote it received, but we are living with the consequences. Indeed, to a high degree it could be argued that the history of the postconciliar Church is the history of the fallout from the failure of *Lumen Gentium* to get the balance right. To examine this issue in a little more depth, we turn now to a closer look at how collegiality has worked in the years since the Council, and especially during the long years of John Paul II's pontificate.

---

[8] Cindy Wooden, "Pope Removes Bishop Who Expressed Openness to Ordaining Women," *National Catholic Reporter*, May 2, 2011, http://ncronline.org/news /women-religious/pope-removes-bishop-who-expressed-openness-ordaining -women.

Chapter 2

The Fate of Collegiality
in the Postconciliar Church

For all the criticisms of John Paul II practice of collegiality, there is no doubt that he spoke often and highly of its importance. From his very first "Urbi et Orbi" address, given the day after his election, where he spoke of the "special bond, that is, collegiality," which "binds together the sacred pastors" (1978), to his fine words on the "synodal dimension of the church" as an expression of "the collegiality of the entire episcopate" (1994), to his relatively late letter (*motu proprio*) on episcopal conferences, *Apostolos Suos* (1998), the collegiality of the bishops was a thread running through his pontificate. Over and over again he wrote of the special bond that existed among the bishops, less often perhaps of the roles that they played together in leading the universal church. Clearly, collegiality was important to John Paul. But what did he mean by *collegiality*? Was his view consistent with the teaching of the Council or the convictions of his brother bishops? There is a possibly apocryphal anecdote told of him on the day of his inauguration as pope. Immediately after the ceremony, so the story goes, he turned to Cardinal Léon Joseph Suenens, a leading progressive voice in the Church at the time, rubbed his hands together gleefully, and proclaimed, "And now for some real collegiality!" But what for John Paul was the *real* in "real collegiality"?

Although John Paul spoke and wrote long and often about collegiality, his failures in this regard were probably the most frequently mentioned item in the more critical assessments of his legacy that appeared at the time of his death. In March 2005 Hans Küng wrote of John Paul's acceptance of Vatican II's call for collegiality but added that "he disregarded the collegiality which had been agreed to there and instead celebrated the triumph of his papacy at the cost of the bishops."[1] Thomas Groome of Boston College said that "there are serious aspects of the council that it would seem as if this man did not embrace and implement; for example, the call to collegiality."[2] The influential Cardinal Franz König wrote at length on this topic, opining at one point that:

> The Second Vatican Council, by linking its doctrine of collegiality to that of papal primacy as defined at Vatican I, gave us a precise description of the significance of the Episcopal college and of its tasks in conjunction with the Petrine office. One could call it an act of divine providence, in order better to meet the new requirements for the world church. In fact, however, de facto and not de jure, intentionally or unintentionally, the curia authorities working in conjunction with the pope have appropriated the tasks of the episcopal college. It is they who now carry out almost all of them.[3]

And even the deliberately centrist Rome correspondent of the lay-run US *National Catholic Reporter*, John Allen, commented that "whatever may be said publicly, John Paul II did not endear himself to some of his brother bishops . . . in the exercise of collegiality."[4]

From the very first moment of the Council to the last, and of course beyond, collegiality has never stopped being a controversial idea. While on the surface it sounds a clear democratizing note, drawing the bishops together into greater responsibility for the governance of the universal Church, it is also susceptible of a more conservative turn. It is quite possible to see the bishops' role in ecclesial governance as little more than their expression of solidarity with the papal voice. Collegiality was one of the principal issues at the Council in face of which the battle lines were drawn up between the majority

---

[1] Hans Küng "The Pope's Contradictions," Der Spegel (March 25, 2005), available most conveniently in English at http://www.spiegel.de/international/Spiegel/0,1518,348471,00.html.

[2] PBS, "Considering the Papacy of John Paul II (April 1, 2005), http://www.pbs.org/newshour/bb/religion/jan-june05/pope_4-01.html.

[3] Franz Cardinal König, "My Vision for the Church of the Future," *The Tablet* (March 27, 1999).

[4] "He Was a Magnificent Pope Who Presided over a Controversial Pontificate," *National Catholic Reporter* (April 4, 2005).

of the bishops and the "curial party," bent on maintaining centralized control over the universal Church.[5] It is an idea whose ramifications spill over into the wider notion of "coresponsibility," in which not only bishops but priests and even the laity come to share collective accountability for the shape and fate of the church.[6] It is both an important corrective to the old standoff in church history between the papalists and the conciliarists, and it was intended to help balance the papal overemphasis of Vatican I. It seems not to have succeeded to any great extent in either intent.

John XXIII and Paul VI on Collegiality

It is instructive to begin the examination of John Paul II's under-standing of collegiality by briefly examining the ways in which his immediate predecessors in office fostered collegiality. John XXIII and Paul VI seem to have had discernibly different attitudes. In his outstanding biography of Pope Paul VI, Peter Hebblethwaite contrasts the approaches of John XXIII and Paul VI to collegiality as "from below" and "from above."[7] John XXIII, the architect of Vatican II, died in May 1963, before the notion of collegiality had come to oc-cupy center stage in the deliberations of the Council fathers, but

---

[5] It is also true that further battle lines have been drawn up over whether or not this well-rehearsed drama of the Council is an accurate depiction. However, those with little to gain from any distortion seem to agree that from the first moment John XXIII called the Council, perhaps even to the present day, the Vatican Curia have been mostly dead set against it. The most readable version of these events remains Xavier Rynne's articles for *The New Yorker*, subsequently published in book form and now available in a one-volume edition, *Vatican Council II* (Maryknoll, NY: Orbis, 1999). The most authoritative source is the magisterial five-volume *History of Vatican II* (Maryknoll, NY: Orbis, 2000–2006), eds. Giuseppe Alberigo and Joseph A. Komon-chak. For those with less time, money, or stamina, Alberigo has also authored *A Brief History of Vatican II* (Maryknoll, NY: Orbis, 2006). Two other vital resources are John O'Malley's *What Happened at Vatican II* and Yves Congar's *My Journal of the Council*. For a sample of the opposite point of view, albeit a rather extreme and intemperate version, see Ralph M. McInerney, *What Went Wrong with Vatican II: The Catholic Crisis Explained* (Manchester, NH: Sophia Institute Press, 1998).

[6] The *locus classicus* here is Léon Joseph Suenens, *Coresponsibility in the Church*, trans. Francis Martin (New York: Herder and Herder, 1968). Suenen's autobiography adds material of interest: *Memories and Hopes* (Dublin: Veritas, 1992).

[7] Peter Hebblethwaite, *Paul VI: The First Modern Pope* (New York: Paulist, 1993), 352.

several hints suggest a more generous understanding of episcopal coresponsibility than was later demonstrated in the extraordinarily cautious reign of his successor, Paul VI. In their two approaches we can see the battle lines drawn up, long before there even seemed to be a battle to fight. Both by temperament and conviction, the two pontiffs held differing views of the Church and, so, of the place of the bishops in church governance.

When John XXIII convoked the Second Vatican Council, he did not see it as the completion of its 1870 predecessor but as a fundamentally new Council, indeed a "new Pentecost."[8] While he was responsible for giving the Vatican Curia a major role in preparations for the Council, he may have been surprised and dismayed by their efforts to subvert and control the assembly. During the first session and after, he allowed and even encouraged the insistence of the great body of the bishops that they have a more decisive role in setting both the agenda and the outcomes of the Council. Numerous small but decisive steps, including the increasing prominence the pope gave to more progressive figures like Belgian Cardinal Suenens and Italian Cardinal Giacomo Lercaro, testify to his awareness of the dynamics,[9] as also did his decision not to be present in the council assemblies for fear that he would inhibit freedom of speech. It was with his encouragement and under his watch that toward the end of the first session the bishops began to discuss the questions of ecclesiology that would rapidly come to be accepted as the focus of the Council. It seems likely, though it can never be proven conclusively, that Pope John hoped for a much more proactive role on the part of the world's bishops in decision making in the Church.

When Paul VI was elected to succeed John XXIII in June 1963, he moved rapidly to confirm his commitment to the continuation and completion of Vatican II—sentiments not really surprising in a man who had, as Cardinal Giovanni Montini of Milan, sided clearly with the more progressive majority during the first session. John XXIII evidently had confidence in Montini. It is said that he prayed that Montini would be his successor. In any case, Paul VI supported the bishops in their commitment to collegiality and enthusiastically promoted the idea of the world synod of bishops as a place for col-

---

[8] Alberigo, *A Brief History*, 1–20, esp. p. 19.
[9] Hebblethwaite, *Paul VI*, 300.

legiality to continue to be expressed after the Council had ended. He even planned to erect a new building to house the bishops, perhaps initially imagining a more permanent presence than the form of synod that eventually emerged. He also promised a thorough reform of the Curia—a reform clearly needed if it was to stop thinking of itself as governing the universal church under papal instruction and begin to see itself as the servant of the entire Church. This promise, sincerely meant, was never fulfilled, though he certainly took important steps to internationalize its membership.

While Paul VI was indeed a man of the Council, he was also a nervous and cautious individual who sought to win overwhelming "yes" votes for the confirmation of Council documents. As anyone knows who works on such matters, compromise is the only way to achieve this kind of result, and the texts on collegiality in *Lumen Gentium* were no exception. Like the bishops themselves, Paul agonized over just what collegiality might mean, supported the decision to ask the Council fathers to respond to five specific questions to clarify their concerns, and—as we saw—issued on his own authority a *nota praevia* explaining and, some said, undercutting the intentions of *Lumen Gentium*.[10] However, the explanatory note—which stressed and repeated the words of the Council fathers themselves that episcopal collegiality was always exercised *cum Petro et sub Petro*—was neither included in the final text nor voted on by the bishops, which gives support to those who consider it simply a political sop to the Curia in search of that overwhelmingly positive vote. Of course, this kind of maneuvering provided ammunition for later efforts to paint Paul VI as a weak and vacillating pontiff who did not really support the conciliar expression of collegiality, just as it could be used to support minimalist interpretations of collegiality adduced on other grounds.

Collegiality in *Lumen Gentium*

During the second session of the Council, the commission drafting the text of *Lumen Gentium* came directly to the bishops with five questions for clarification. The structure of Council debates, with none of the to and fro of the parliamentary system, made it very difficult to determine who spoke for whom and thus what the true feelings of

---

[10] Flannery, ed., *Vatican Council II: The Basic Sixteen Documents*, 92–95.

the majority were. Four of the five questions dealt directly with collegiality, and in their responses the bishops overwhelmingly agreed that episcopal consecration is the highest degree of sacred orders, that each bishop becomes a member of the college by virtue of his consecration, that together with the pope and never without him the college of bishops exercises "full and supreme authority in the church," and that the bishops enjoy this power by divine right. Voting as they did, the conciliar majority clearly scotched more conservative efforts to insist that episcopal authority and thus membership of the college is by delegation from the pope. And in that same month of October 1963, the bishops sent the text of *Lumen Gentium* back to the commission with instructions to reverse the order of chapters 2 and 3, thus placing the discussion of the people of God ahead of that of the hierarchy. These decisive acts set fast the Council's ruling vision of the Church as the baptized, priestly people of God.

A complex and nuanced understanding of collegiality is laid out in *Lumen Gentium*, evidently influenced by the results of the direct questionnaire to which the bishops had responded so clearly. The bishops, successors of the apostles (21), form an episcopal order with "a collegiate character and structure," and into which they enter "in virtue of the sacramental consecration." Together with their head, the pope, and never without him, the bishops "have supreme and full authority over the universal church" (22). Bishops exercise pastoral care over their own dioceses but should also have concern for the universal church. "Each bishop represents his own church" and together with the pope they "represent the whole church in a bond of peace, love and unity" (23). They have the responsibility to teach (24), to preach (25), to be stewards of the Eucharist (26), and to govern their particular Church (27). As teachers, they "proclaim infallibly the doctrine of Christ" when acting in communion with one another and with the pope; "even though dispersed throughout the world," they "are in agreement that a particular teaching is to be held definitively" (25).

If the understanding of collegiality spelled out in *Lumen Gentium* is complex and subtle, it is not always crystal clear. This much is evident: the bishops exercise the fullness of collegiality in acting, in concert and together with the pope, either in an ecumenical council or when all speak with one voice, at the wish of the pope or at least in a way that the pope can "receive." Well and good. But there are other ways in which collegiality is also somehow expressed, as when they assist one another or somehow show their concern for the whole Church, or indeed when they speak in *fora*, such as at episcopal conferences. In all these cases they are not, of course, acting with one voice, nor necessarily at the behest of the pope. These forms of collegiality are real but, to borrow the words of the *nota praevia*, they are not "in full act"—that is, somehow not representative of the fullness of collegiality.[11] This distinction will be important in examining John Paul II's particular understanding of collegiality. This indeed is the crux of the issue. No one would wish to deny that the fullest expression of collegiality lies in just such collective acts of judgment, in Council or not. But the question is whether there is something more, perhaps something less formal, but something that nevertheless gives greater voice to the bishops than they had previously had.

While it is evident that episcopal collegiality is deemed to be an important characteristic of the Church, *Lumen Gentium* never makes it entirely clear whether collegiality is in service of primacy or primacy in service of collegiality. Is the collegial action of the bishops envisaged as a support to the work of the supreme pontiff, bringing solidarity and affirmation of unity to his pronouncements, or is it that the pope is the symbol and focus of the unity of the bishops scattered around the world? Is episcopal collegiality simply a powerful symbol of the unity of the worldwide Church, or is it a mechanism through which the bishops can exercise some element of shared governance? It is hard to avoid the impression that John XXIII would have welcomed assistance in governance, that some at least of the Council fathers would have favored it (Suenens, König, and others), and that Paul VI was wary of any real power sharing at the level of the universal church. And while John Paul I had so little time, there are interesting words in his "Urbi et Orbi" address in August 1978, where he calls on the college of bishops, seeking their "collaboration in the government of the universal Church."[12] It is exactly this

[11] On the general issue of collegiality relative to the authority of episcopal conferences, see the excellent discussion by Joseph A. Komonchak, "The Roman Working Paper on Episcopal Conferences," chap. 6 of *Episcopal Conferences: Historical, Canonical and Theological Studies*, ed. Thomas J. Reese (Washington, DC: Georgetown University Press, 1989).

[12] John Paul I, Address of His Holiness (August 27, 1978), http://www.vatican.va /holy_father/john_paul_i/messages/documents/hf_jp-i_mes_urbi-et-orbi_27081978 _en.html.

emphasis on shared governance that is notable by its absence in the words and especially the deeds of his successor.

John Paul II on Collegiality

Just a few weeks after his predecessor's short-lived papacy, it was John Paul II's turn to present his "Urbi et Orbi" address. The theme of his message was fidelity to the Second Vatican Council, in which he singled out ecclesiological issues for special focus. In particular, "the special bond, that is, collegiality, which 'with Peter and under Peter' binds together the sacred Pastors."

> In order that we may become better informed and more vigilant in undertaking our duty, we particularly urge a deeper reflection on the implications of the collegial bond. By collegiality the Bishops are closely linked with the successor of the blessed Peter, and all collaborate in order to fulfill the high offices committed to them: offices of enlightening the whole People of God with the light of the Gospel, of sanctifying them with the means of grace, of guiding them with pastoral skill.[13]

With hindsight, this programmatic statement is both ironic and informative. Ironic because the failure to implement "the collegial bond" is one of the most frequent criticisms of John Paul's pontificate. And informative because the collaboration to which the pope refers specifies only those roles that the bishops fulfill within the boundaries of their own dioceses—teaching, sanctification, and pastoral care. The plea for the assistance of shared governance that his predecessor had made is not present.

Throughout his lengthy pontificate, John Paul II returned frequently to the topic of collegiality. Nowhere was this more illuminating than in his Holy Thursday 1979 letter to the bishops, so early in his tenure as pope, where he makes a distinction that will come to mark his thinking on the topic:

> We must express the wish, today especially, that everything that the Second Vatican Council so wonderfully renewed in our awareness should take on an ever more mature character

[13] John Paul II, Address of His Holiness (October 17, 1978), http://www.vatican.va /holy_father/john_paul_ii/speeches/1978/documents/hf_jp-ii_spe_19781017_primo -radiomessaggio_en.html.

of collegiality, both as the principle of our collaboration (*colle-gialitas effectiva*) and as the character of a cordial fraternal bond (*collegialitas affectiva*), in order to build up the Mystical Body of Christ and to deepen the unity of the whole People of God.[14]

Effective collegiality refers to the principle in virtue of which the bishops can speak collectively in Council or with the pope, sharing indeed in a certain infallibility. They always act with Peter and under Peter. And "Peter" could always do alone, it would seem, what they in fact are doing together.[15] But *affective* collegiality is the bond of solidarity within the episcopal college. Much later, toward the end of his pontificate, John Paul attempted to clarify the meaning of affective collegiality, referring to it as "'the spirit of collegiality' . . . which is the basis of the Bishops' concern for the other particular Churches and for the universal Church." "Consequently," he continued, "if we must say that a Bishop is never alone, inasmuch as he is always united to the Father through the Son in the Holy Spirit, we must also add that he is also never alone because he is always and continuously united with his brothers in the episcopate and with the one whom the Lord has chosen as the Successor of Peter."[16]

While the distinction between affective and effective collegiality has become common currency in Vatican documents and in the writings of John Paul II in particular, its origins and, indeed, its precise meaning are somewhat mysterious. It seems that it first emerged in the course of the 1969 extraordinary Rome synod, though it does not appear in any documentation from that time. It derives, in all probability, from efforts to clarify the distinction we referred to above between the full exercise of collegiality in formal united pronouncements of the bishops together with the pope and all other "lesser" exercises of collegiality in mutual support, episcopal conferences, and so on. "The spirit of collegiality, or affective collegiality," writes

[14] Pope John Paul II, Letter to Bishops for Holy Thursday (April 8, 1979), http://www.ewtn.com/library/papaldoc/jp2bps79.htm.

[15] So is there a difference, is there some addendum or improvement provided by the act of episcopal solidarity? Is the statement somehow more effective or more acceptable than it would be as the word of the pope alone? If not, what does collegial action add, and what does it mean additionally to the bishop's sense of his role in the universal church?

[16] Pope John Paul II, *Pastores Gregis*, 8, http://www.catholicnewsagency.com/document.php?n=18.

the pope in *Pastores Gregis*, "is always present among the Bishops as *communio episcoporum*, but only in certain acts does it find expression as effective collegiality." "The various ways in which affective collegiality comes to be realized in effective collegiality belong to the human order," he continues, "but in varying degrees they concretize the divine requirement that the episcopate should express itself in a collegial manner."[17]

There is, of course, a value beyond the sheer affectivity of affective collegiality, in that solidarity can be helpful in times of confusion. This is what, in his 1979 encyclical *Redemptoris Hominis*, John Paul seemed to be saying when he commented that affective collegiality "showed itself particularly relevant in the difficult postconciliar period, when the shared unanimous position of the college of the bishops—which displayed, chiefly through the synod, its union with Peter's Successor—helped to dissipate doubts and at the same time indicated the correct ways for renewing the Church in her universal dimension."[18] At this point in the letter John Paul makes supportive references to national episcopal conferences, councils of priests, and diocesan, provincial, and national synods, writing approvingly of lay involvement in synods and pastoral councils. He is clearly placing all such participatory structures in the context of the solidarity and unanimity that should mark the exercise of affective collegiality, an association that should be suggestive about the dearth of effective roles. For if the role of all these groups is in their different ways an exercise of coresponsibility on the part of the whole church, where is the place for the creative contributions that some might think would emerge from different experiences, different roles, different races and genders, and different geographical locations? It would seem that difference of opinion and honest debate or disagreement with papal directives could never be classified as an act of effective collegiality. But might it be that such a to and fro of public debate is one important way in which affective collegiality could and should be exercised? The bond of unity among the bishops in their concern for the universal Church should surely be expected to show itself at times in healthy disagreement about its future direction. Furthermore, if effective collegiality is only fully exercised in speaking with

[17] Ibid.
[18] Pope John Paul II, On Redemption and the Dignity of the Human Race, sec. 5, http://www.ewtn.com/library/encyc/jp2redem.htm.

one voice under the leadership of the pope, it is quite difficult to see what is so "effective" about it.

John Paul II's consistent reliance on the distinction and relationship between affective and effective collegiality is all of a piece with his concern to reassert the importance of centralized ecclesiastical authority. In *Pastores Gregis*, for example, the pope seeks to clarify the meaning of collegiality by drawing an ecclesiological analogy. "A parallelism can thus be established," he writes, "between the Church as one and universal, and therefore indivisible, and the episcopacy as one and indivisible, and therefore universal." The true nature of the parallelism, in John Paul's mind, is that "the principle and foundation" of the unity of the Church or of the body of bishops "is the Roman Pontiff." The universal Church "is not the sum of the particular churches or a federation of the latter" but "precedes creation itself." Just so, the college of bishops "is a reality which precedes the office of being the head of a particular Church." Hence, "just as the universal Church is one and indivisible, so too the College of Bishops is one 'indivisible theological subject,' and hence the supreme, full and universal power possessed by the College, and by the Roman Pontiff personally, is one and indivisible."[19]

The practical significance of this abstruse set of arguments is worth thinking about. In the first instance, it reintroduces the pattern of deductive and ahistorical thinking in and about the Church, which the Council fathers seem to have wanted to eliminate. A putative theological truth (the preexistence of the Church, presumably from all eternity) recognized only much later in history is given hermeneutical privilege over the actual events of history. A more inductive and historically sensitive approach would recognize that the early Church stumbled its way into a pattern of ecclesiastical arrangements over many centuries. While it is perfectly legitimate to reflect theologically on the value of these historical developments, the effort to canonize them by locating them in the mind of Christ flies in the face of sound historical scholarship. It can also lead to some conclusions that are conveniently supportive of the restorationist ecclesial vision. For example, John Paul immediately draws the conclusion from his words quoted above that there are many ways to be bishop,

---

[19] Pope John Paul II, *Pastores Gregis*, 8, quoting himself in *Apostolos Suos*, 12. This 1998 *motu proprio* on the "Theological and Juridical Nature of Episcopal Conferences" can be found at http://www.ewtn.com/library/papaldoc/jp2apost.htm.

and the connection to a geographical area as leader of a local church is only one of them. There are auxiliary bishops and there are others who act as representatives "of the Roman Pontiff in the offices of the Holy See or in Papal Legations." It would seem that we have come a long way from the ancient Church's belief that a bishop was married to his diocese, and while this might well be a legitimate historical development, to justify that development on the grounds that it follows directly from the preexistent church evident in Jesus' establishment of the apostolic college is deeply misleading.

In recognizing the relationship between collegiality and ecclesiology we may be at the heart of John Paul II's seizing upon the obscurity of the affective/effective distinction.[20] That we may also be at the end of the line for any resolution of the argument is one clear lesson of the famed Ratzinger/Kasper debate over the priority of the universal or the local church.[21] This began when Kasper, then-bishop of Rottenburg, Germany, took exception to the statement in a 1992 document from the Congregation for the Doctrine of the Faith (CDF) that the universal church "is not the result of the communion of the Churches, but, in its essential mystery, it is a reality *ontologically and temporally* prior to every *individual* particular Church."[22] While the argument is a complex one, especially as it is further developed in the public exchange between Kasper and Ratzinger, Kasper's principal point is that Vatican II had expressed the relationship between the local and universal church in a way that saw the local church as an expression of the universal Church, indeed the only concrete expression of the universal Church, while the language of "ontological priority" employed by the CDF made the universal Church an abstraction and failed to recognize that it is only real in and through the local churches out of which it was first formed.[23] The core of Ratzinger's response is that the preexistence of the church is attested to by early church fathers (Clement of Rome and the Shepherd of

---

[20] At the end of Komonchak's extraordinarily careful analysis of the distinction (see n. 11 above) he concludes that "the distinction between affective and effective collegiality should be abandoned."

[21] See n. 21 in the introduction of this book.

[22] John Paul II, "Letter to the Bishops of the Catholic Church on Some Aspects of the Church Understood as Communion," par. 9, http://www.catholicnewsagency .com/document.php?n=130.

[23] This point had been made earlier by Komonchak, "On the Authority of Bishops' Conferences," *America* (September 12, 1998): 7–10.

Hermas), and that the preexistent church, like the preexistent Israel of Jewish teaching, is all that preserves ecclesiology from simply seeing the Church as a human organization. Kasper finds the same problem in *Apostolos Suos* and also links it to collegiality, believing that the relationship between the college of bishops together with the pope, and the pope alone, is inadequately expressed. The result is that the authority of the college of bishops may in practice be little more than a "naked fiction," in Kasper's words, since the pope can always act without formally involving the college.

The larger problem with John Paul's understanding of episcopal collegiality is that it does not seem to be faithful to the conciliar intent, though as we have seen there is a measure of ambiguity in the expression of that intent, which could enable the claim that it is indeed quite faithful. The Council clearly wished to stress the joint responsibility of all the bishops for the governance of the universal Church and used the term collegiality to emphasize the collective authority of the world's bishops, together with the pope as the symbol of their unity and the unity of the Church. Collegiality was expressed as a Spirit-filled joint responsibility for the good of the universal Church. The only "effective" role the bishops assigned themselves was in the solemn arena of an ecumenical council. Beyond that, they were content to leave in a healthily fuzzy condition the juridical dimensions of collegiality. However, the curial mentality that was always at war with the pastoral intentions of the Council could not be happy with such ambiguity, and thus was born the contorted relationship between affective and effective collegiality. John Paul's restorationism seized on the distinction and assured the triumph of that stratagem.

One of the most thoughtful discussions of the meaning of collegiality was provided by John R. Quinn, retired archbishop of San Francisco, responding to John Paul II's encyclical letter on Commitment to Ecumenism, *Ut unum sint.*[24] John Paul famously raised the question of how the papacy might be reformed to become more clearly "a service of love recognized by all concerned," and Quinn's book-length answer includes a substantial chapter on collegiality and the papacy. Quinn writes that the central issue is to "enshrine

[24] Pope John Paul II, That They May Be One (May 25, 1995), http://www.newadvent.org/library/docs_jp02uu.htm. Archbishop Quinn's book is *The Reform of the Papacy: The Costly Call to Christian Unity* (New York: Crossroad, 1999).

the convergence of primacy and collegiality affirmed in balanced tension." He finds the source for this in the support Pius IX gave to the German bishops when they insisted against Chancellor Otto von Bismarck that Vatican I had not made the pope an absolute sovereign. They were clear that they could "decisively refute the statement that the bishops have become by reason of the Vatican decrees mere papal functionaries with no personal responsibility." In contrast to this healthy understanding of their reciprocal relations, an understanding with which Vatican II is fully consistent, Quinn is distressed by the poor practice of collegiality since the Council, specifically in the challenges mounted by Ratzinger and Jerome Hamer to the status of episcopal conferences and on the synods of bishops, which he considers to have been "a great disappointment."

The synod of bishops established by Paul VI during the final sessions of the Council was proclaimed at the time to be a prime instrument of episcopal collegiality. Even during Paul VI's reign it became clear that it would be no such thing, and John Paul II continued in the fiction that real collegiality was enacted there. The synod is called by the pope, the topic of discussion is determined by the pope, items that may not be discussed are indicated by the pope, and the conversations and deliberations of the bishops are not made public, at least in theory, but rather handed over to the pope for his personal use as he prepares a document on the synod's theme. The postsynodal apostolic exhortation published in the pope's name ostensibly owes much to the bishops' work, but it is impossible to tell how much this is true, since their final "propositions" are never made public. Quinn adds three further problems with the synods: they include members of the Roman Curia, they all take place in Rome, and the structure of the meetings requires formal prepared statements without the opportunity of responding to one another after the manner of a healthy debate.

The synod of bishops under the papacy of John Paul II was not, to say the least, a shining example of what it had been created to be. It was neither effective collegiality, since the bishops simply advised in private, nor a particularly good demonstration of affective collegiality, since its structure belies the trust that is supposed to reside in the affective bond. Collegiality in this way becomes an instrument of centralization, just as it is profoundly alienating to the bishops' sense of themselves as a college, engaged collectively in responsible leadership of the universal Church. Collegiality becomes hegemonic, and a bishop exercising his collegial responsibilities at the Rome synod is trapped in that classic hegemonic snare of embracing his own oppression. Sometimes bishops say they are powerless, and our response might be to smile. But in many ways they are, and not a little of this is attributable to the manner in which the conciliar understanding of collegiality has been converted to the service of curial centralization. In this denial of the meaning of Vatican II, enwrapped as it is in theological abstractions about the preexistence of the universal Church, John Paul II is not innocent. Much of the theoretical justification for this particular reading of collegiality may have been the work of Ratzinger as prefect of the Congregation for the Doctrine of the Faith. But most of it happened on John Paul's watch, and much of it is published in documents that bear his signature. It is, moreover, exactly what one could expect of a man of John Paul's temperament, impatient with the democratic process and strongly convinced of being personally guided by the Spirit and protected by the Virgin. What possible need could he have had for shared governance?

In the end, perhaps, John Paul II's version of collegiality is guided by and explicable partially in terms of his personality, partially through his personal history. Even those least impressed by his teaching are in no doubt that he was a profoundly charismatic leader. Why else would young people completely uninterested in his conservative ethical and doctrinal positions travel halfway across the world to bask in his presence? In his prime as pope, John Paul was obviously warm and welcoming, seemingly sometimes verging on the sentimental, always ready with the expressive smile and the warm hug. He appeared genuinely to love the crowds, the people of God—especially those who were "poor or afflicted in any way"— and his brother bishops. But he never gave an inch on any of the profoundly centralizing governance style nor in the traditional cast of his theological opinions. His vision of the Church was of a deeply affective community under strong, centralized effective leadership. This leadership was strengthened, he seemed to say, through the affective bond of unity of the bishops, teaching and believing in solidarity with the bishop of Rome. And here is where the personal history combines with the personality to render him inflexible. The role of the papacy in John Paul's understanding is deeply influenced by the role of the Polish Church under communism. Strong centralized leadership was essential in protecting the Church in Poland, which was itself an expression of protection for the Polish people. Open exchanges and difference of opinion would have been interpreted as weakness and would have weakened the Church. Sadly, John Paul II had absolutely no personal experience of life in a democratic political environment where frank and open public exchange of views is reasonably accounted a sign of the health of the community. Had he been the product of a different world, he might have found more of a place for truly effective collegiality.

From Cardinal Ratzinger to Benedict XVI: Collegiality Today

If John Paul's version of collegiality was a function largely of his temperament and style, that of Joseph Ratzinger was grounded much more in an intellectual conviction about the proper interpretation of Vatican II. As Kevin McKenna pointed out in a December 10, 2007, article in *America* magazine, Benedict understood collegiality not so much as power sharing but rather involving "the bishops collectively in the formation of policy on major questions." He is not a fan of the synods of bishops, partially because they tend to suggest a greater role in governance than he believes individual bishops possess. Confirming his lack of enthusiasm, Benedict acted to reduce the length of the first synod during his pontificate (in 2005) from four weeks to three. As David Gibson commented, for Benedict, decentralization is not about extending more of a role in governance to the bishops but rather "about the bishops making decisions the way Rome wanted so that Rome did not have to do so for them."[25] The same cautious mentality is in evidence in the then-Cardinal Ratzinger's suspicion of the role of national bishops' conferences. He worried both that they could become a kind of alternative magisterium and that they undermined the authority of the individual bishop in his own diocese. And he also made clear that the main purpose of all such synodal gatherings was not taking votes but "conscience formation."

In their recent book, *The Ratzinger Reader*,[26] Lieven Boeve and Gerard Mannion offer a reading of Pope Benedict's career that, in general, challenges the common assumption that he had grown more

---

[25] David Gibson, *The Rule of Benedict: Pope Benedict XVI and His Battle with the Modern World* (San Francisco: HarperSanFrancisco, 2006), 302.

[26] *The Ratzinger Reader: Mapping a Theological Journey*, ed. Lieven Boeve and Gerard Mannion (London and New York: T & T Clark, 2010).

conservative over the years in favor of a reading of his work that suggests essential continuity. Gerard Mannion's editorial observations in the section of the book on "Teaching and Authority"[27] show that at the time of Vatican II, Joseph Ratzinger had serious doubts about the wisdom of the *nota praevia* that was attached to the text of *Lumen Gentium* and that his early essay in the very first issue of *Concilium*[28] was very supportive of collegiality. However, Mannion adjudges this an exception to a more cautious position, one indeed leaning a little more toward papal authority than episcopal collegiality, evidenced in the more recent thought of Ratzinger and, indeed, of Pope Benedict. While Ratzinger in the early sixties seemed consistently to recognize the interdependence of papacy and episcopacy, more recent writings on the role of the synod of bishops reveal a sensibility not that different from that of his predecessor. The synod, he says, cannot be "a genuine organ of the episcopal college" because "the college's right to govern cannot be delegated." One can sense the proximity of the affective/effective distinction in the cardinal's conclusion that the primary concern of the synod cannot be expanding its own rights "over against central Roman authorities that appear to be far too powerful" but should rather be attention to "our common work on behalf of the gospel."[29]

---

[27] Ibid., 179–223.

[28] Cardinal Joseph Ratzinger, "The Pastoral Implications of Episcopal Collegiality," *Concilium* 1 (Glen Rock, NJ: Paulist, 1964): 39–67.

[29] Ibid., 207.

Chapter 3

Episcopal Leadership
in the American Church Today

Who would be a bishop in our Church today? With the best will in the world, with purity of intention and bereft of ecclesial ambition, any bishop is bogged down with administrative responsibilities that make it very difficult to be an effective successor of the apostles. The continuing fallout from the scandal of sex abuse, problems with those few clergy who are embezzlers, alcoholics, or philanderers, the need to close schools or parishes because of dwindling enrollment and the ever-present need to maintain revenue sources that keep the work of the local church going are all sources of anxiety that have little or nothing to do with preaching the Gospel. This is all a far cry from the picture of the bishop laid out in *Lumen Gentium* and discussed in chapter 1 of this book. Here in full is one of the finest statements the document made of its vision of the bishop:

> Sent as he is by the Father to govern his family, a bishop should keep before his eyes the example of the Good Shepherd, who came not to be served but to serve and to lay down his life for his sheep. Taken from among human beings and subject to weakness himself, he can sympathise with those who are ignorant and erring. He should not refuse to listen to his subjects whose welfare he promotes as of his very own children and whom he urges to collaborate readily with him. Destined to render an account for their souls to God, by prayer, preaching and all good works of charity he should be solicitous both for their welfare and also for that of those who do not yet belong to the one flock, all of whom he should regard as entrusted to him in the Lord. Since, like St. Paul, he is in duty bound to everyone, he should

be eager to preach the Gospel to all, and to spur his faithful on
to apostolic and missionary activity. (27)

The work of the bishop, think the Council fathers, is notable for
the depth of its human concern and the awful responsibility he has
for the spiritual welfare of those under his charge, indeed even for
those within the geographical ambit of his local church who are not
members of the community of faith. There is nothing here about
administrative duties. Instead, the bishop is perceived primarily as
an animator of the lives and work of all the faithful. His wise governance is intimately connected to preaching the Gospel, which *Lumen
Gentium* says has "pride of place" among the duties of the bishop (25).
There can surely be little doubt that most of our bishops strive to do
this, that most of them find their bureaucratic responsibilities make
this harder, and that most of them would dearly love to be left alone
to be simply the spiritual leader of the local church.

One of the consequences of the bishop being too heavily involved
in administration and too little in direct pastoral leadership is that
it is all too easy to come to think of oneself as "governing" in ways
much closer to secular models than to those of the Gospel. In the
Christian community, episcopal power is a gift of the Holy Spirit for
the purpose of empowering the people of God to pursue their baptismal priesthood in the world. This power is seriously misused when
it substitutes for or preempts the prophetic role of the whole people.
In part 2 of this book we will turn more directly to an examination
of what it means for the people of God to exercise their prophetic
responsibility. For now it is sufficient to note that these responsibilities are those of all the baptized. Bishops preach the Gospel; the laity
are the primary actors of the Church in the world.

It has lately been a particular characteristic of the American episcopate that it has become more rather than less intrusive in public
affairs. This has happened in part because at least some of the bishops
believe that our pluralistic American society is a genuine threat to the
freedom to live out the Gospel message. Whether this is an accurate
assessment or a simple misperception, it is not immediately obvious
that it is the responsibility of the bishops to step beyond their role as
proclaimers of the Gospel and animators of the people of God to take
up the challenge of secular society. Vatican II surely considered this to
be the job of the laity, acting as individuals in virtue of their baptism,
not delegates of the hierarchy. This picture certainly does not preclude

a role for the bishops in proclaiming Church teaching, especially in the area of doctrine, but it argues for a less prominent role than they seem to have been trying to exercise in recent American public debate.

Pluralistic societies such as our own present the Church with the need to balance the concern for legitimate religious freedom with the restraint that is appropriate when we are only one voice in society, albeit a loud one. Currently in the United States we have a Church divided within itself, divided in its attitude and loyalty to its leaders, and whose leaders are themselves often in contentious positions vis-à-vis the state and civil society. This is not a healthy situation, nor is it the inevitable result of the need for the Church to "stand up to" secular society or "secular humanism" or "pluralism." A Church so conceived is failing to recognize the true nature of the Church/world relationship and perhaps even moving dangerously close to the evils of "integrism" as Rahner defined it—namely, the effort to impose the teachings of the Church as a kind of blueprint or ethical template on the secular world. What must be sought, on the contrary, is a different role for the Church vis-à-vis the world, one in which the Church appropriately influences civil society without giving in to the temptation to "integrism." One, in fact, far closer to the vision of partnership and reciprocal learning that distinguished Vatican II's *Gaudium et Spes*. There may be a clue to the way forward in the simple observation that in this Pastoral Constitution on the Church in the World of Today, the longest of all the Council documents, there are only four references to bishops.

In recent years there have been a number of prominent examples of strong positions on political issues taken by the bishops. A long-standing concern that has resurfaced periodically around the time of major elections has been the vexed question of when, if ever, it is appropriate to withhold or threaten to withhold the Eucharist from Catholic politicians considered "soft" on the Church's sternly pro-life position on abortion. Here, indeed, we have seen more or less public disagreement between bishops, with the then-Archbishop Raymond Burke declaring that "the person who persists publicly in grave sin is to be denied Holy Communion, and it [Canon Law] doesn't say that the bishop shall decide this. It's an absolute,"[1] while Cardinal

---

[1] Hilary White, "Vatican Official: Bishops Have No Choice but to Refuse Communion to Pro-Abort Politicians" (February 4, 2009), http://www.lifesitenews.com/ldn/2009/feb/09020402.html.

Donald Wuerl countered with the statement that "we never—the Church just didn't use Communion this way. It wasn't a part of the way we do things, and it wasn't a way we convinced Catholic politicians to appropriate the faith and live it and apply it; the challenge has always been to convince people."[2] This particular issue did not surface much, if at all, in the 2012 elections and would in any case have been overshadowed by the bishops' fury over the Health and Human Services mandate to require health insurance to include coverage for contraception, which was transformed into a more general concern that religious freedom was itself under threat.[3]

In public policy issues, is there a line over which the bishops ought not to step? A positive response to this question is most often based on the judgment that the Church might endanger its tax-free status by inserting itself into political controversies, especially if it seems to be uttering veiled threats about how Catholics should or should not, might or might not, vote. There is, however, a more fundamental theological reason for being wary of these practices. It goes to the question of the relationship between the way the grace of God works in and through the Church, and the way in which God's grace is differently present in and through the complexity of the secular world itself. Whenever the Church seems to be proposing its own ethical standpoint as a template for secular society there are reasons to hesitate, not because the Church's positions are wrong, but because the workings of God's grace in the secular world needs to be respected, and the world is not under the jurisdiction of the Church.

The Church is present in the world somewhat differently, depending on whether we focus on the institutional, hierarchical Church or on the living witness of individual Catholics. While, of course, the Church in the first sense is in the world as an historically bound, visible reality, changing its form and its manner of operation across the centuries, interacting with monarchs and democratically elected leaders, and indeed inevitably colored by the times in which it happens to be living,

---

[2] Melinda Henneberger, "Wuerl: Why I Won't Deny Pelosi Communion," *Politics Daily* (May 6, 2009), http://www.politicsdaily.com/2009/05/06/archbishop-wuerl-why-I-won-t-deny-pelosi-communion.

[3] The US Catholic Bishops' website presents the official position (http://www.usccb.org/issues-and-action/religious-liberty/). Cathleen Kaveny has a good discussion from a different perspective in her article, "Is the Government 'Defining Religion'?: The Bishops' Case against the Mandate," *Commonweal* (January 25, 2013).

this historical presence of the Church does not of itself even begin to exhaust the meaning of "the community and sacrament of salvation." The Church as sacrament is only as efficacious as its individual members are faith-filled and loving witnesses to the Gospel. So, thinking about apostolic activity, the Church/world relationship is between the secular world and the baptized Christians who live and work within it. While the institutional Church exercises its prophetic function by teaching at some level of abstraction, the baptized Christian, lay or ordained, lives out her or his prophetic call in baptism by teaching through concrete actions and decisions in the secular world. What this might suggest for the consideration of Catholic public officials and their access to the Eucharist is that while the Church enunciates principles, the real teaching is done in the example of holy living offered by the individual Christian, including those public officials struggling openly with the tension between differing responsibilities. Another, more traditional, way to say this is that the effective ministry of the Church to the world is in direct correlation with the degree to which individual Catholics translate that teaching into apostolic activity. This is partially a matter of education and courage, and partially subject to the realities of ecclesial reception of teaching. In any given instance of failure, the balance between the blind or willful ignorance of the Catholic community and the ineffectualness or even the erroneous character of the teaching is a matter for debate and discernment.

The saving presence of the Church in the world is to be found in the Church as the community of believers and in the lives and witness of individual believers, not in the Church as Church, which, as what James Alison has called "the regime and discipline of signs," can only be effective in and through the ways in which believers enflesh these signs in history, signs "aimed at summoning forth certain shapes of human desire, interpretation, and living together, rather than coercing people into sacred structures."[4] The challenge to the Church is to rid itself of everything that impedes its sign value; the challenge for the baptized is to act in history in faithful witness to the sign that is the Church, both the sign of the cross and the sign of the reign of God. The Church is always present as the regime of signs, but the sign becomes sacrament only in the lives of Christians. The

---

[4] James Alison, "Sacrifice, Law and the Catholic Faith: Is Secularity Really the Enemy?" *The Tablet* (lecture, London, December 2006), http://www.jamesalison .co.uk/pdf/eng36.pdf.

temptation of the Church, always needing to be countered by the praxis of believers, is to see itself as a system of goodness and thus to place law and ethics ahead of the nourishment of faith in the Gospel.

For an interesting example of a very different approach offered by one of the more prominent members of the US hierarchy, we can turn to the words of Archbishop Charles Chaput in his 2010 address to Baptist ministers in Houston on the fiftieth anniversary of John F. Kennedy's famous effort, also in Houston, to explain how he as a Catholic president would manage his responsibilities to a pluralistic American society.[5] Chaput was deeply critical of Kennedy's effort, as he describes it, to drive a deep wedge between his Catholic conscience and his duties as president. Chaput recognized the justice of Kennedy's famous remark that if he was forced into a position where his conscience differed from what was expected of him as president, then he would resign the presidency. But despite this, Chaput sees in Kennedy a kind of prototype of the Catholic politician today who, in Chaput's judgment, employs a fundamentally dualistic approach to being a Catholic in public life, whereas—Chaput argues—one cannot simply divorce one's most deeply held religious convictions from one's responsibilities in public service. Kennedy's insistence on the absolute wall of separation between religion and politics was not only a misperception of the constitution and a misunderstanding of the Catholic position but also, in effect, a secularization of the presidency in order to win, argued Chaput. The result was a more or less complete privatization of religious belief, and that has had very serious consequences for American culture and politics, the archbishop thinks, most of all in the federal law that legalized abortion. "As a nation," he said, "we might profitably ask ourselves whom and what we've really been worshipping in our 40 million 'legal' abortions since 1973."[6]

While it would be sheer folly to disagree with Chaput's principal contention in his 2008 book, *Render unto Caesar*, that Catholics are often neither sufficiently well-informed nor courageous enough to represent faithfully the integrity of Catholic life and belief, there are

[5] The full text of this speech is available at http://www.ewtn.com/library /BISHOPS/chapxianpublife.HTM. In most respects it summarizes and reprises positions laid out in much more detail in Charles Chaput's book, *Render unto Caesar: Serving the Nation by Living Our Catholic Belief in Public Life* (New York: Doubleday, 2008).

[6] On Kennedy as "the first Baptist president," see Charles Chaput, *Render unto Caesar*, 133–37.

certainly some places where disagreement is possible. This is particularly the case when we ask about strategies for evangelization,
and what they might imply for an understanding of the Church/
world relationship. To what degree, additionally, might it be the
responsibility of the teaching Church that its faithful members are
somehow deficient in knowledge or courage? Certainly, if Catholics
are ignorant of the teachings of the Church it must at least in part
be a failure of the teachers and cannot simply be blamed on blind
or willful ignorance. And is it perhaps possible that their putative
lack of courage is really a judgment about the degree to which they
fail simply to mirror the positions of the institutional Church? Is a
Catholic only courageous when reflecting the teaching of the Church
and inevitably cowardly when not quite "getting it"? Are there not
possibly some occasions when "dissent" points to inadequacy in the
teachings, or at least in their manner of presentation?[7]

Chaput's position on the Church/world relationship is very forceful. The danger of this kind of approach is that while it can on the
one hand arrogate to itself too much of the legitimate responsibilities
of baptized Christians to be the presence of the Church in the secular
world, it can also too easily become unintentionally entangled with
a negative and disapproving evaluation of the world itself. There is
surely something overstated, for example, in Chaput's argument
that the "modern" separation of Church and state doctrine "has explicitly anti-Catholic roots in the nineteenth century," that "it grew
directly out of bigotry," and that "it began in a bald effort to wall
Catholics out of the nation's public life."[8] Even if there is a measure
of truth here, given some of the frankly unproductive attitudes of the
nineteenth-century papacy toward church and state issues, it is not
surprising that suspicion of Catholics was rife in the young American
democracy. His view seems unduly negative. He sometimes fails to
recognize that grace is at work in and through the secular world
and that this graceful presence of God in the world is not simply a
reflection of the grace of God in the Church. Chaput writes:

[7] It is a pedagogical truism that poor teachers blame their students while good
teachers look for another way to enlighten the classroom darkness. I will return to
this idea several times in the remainder of the book.

[8] Chaput, *Render unto Caesar*, 185–86.

In our legitimate hopes for a role in American life, Catholics
have ignored an unpleasant truth: that there are active, motivated groups in modern American society that bitterly resent
the Catholic Church and the Christian Gospel, and would like to
silence both. . . . Many Catholics since Vatican II have recoiled
almost instinctively from traditional images of "the church militant." But like it or not, that is exactly what we are—or should
be. We are in a struggle for the souls of our people and our country. We ignore this at our own peril. We also fail as disciples.[9]

Behind the rhetorical exaggerations of Chaput's words there does lie
a much more substantial approach to the Church/world relationship.
The key is to be found in Chaput's awareness that in the end politics
is not what the Church is about. Surely there is an institutional side
to Church life, and it is undoubtedly correct that Christian involvement in political life, especially lay Christians, is one important way
that the Gospel vision of human flourishing is promoted. But the
most effective form of evangelization is the "personal contact and
friendship" that reveals that "the Catholic faith is more than a set of
principles we agree to, but rather an entirely new way of life. . . .
People must see that new life being lived. They must see the joy that
it brings. They must see the union of the believer with Jesus Christ."[10]
This is an altogether happier ecclesiological orientation than one in
which the bishops are constantly fixating on political life.

Karl Rahner is quite helpful in formulating how believing Christians can live one life, as a Christian in the world, not two, as a
Christian and a person of the world.[11] His Church and world essays
written at the time of the Council and in the years immediately after
it are suffused with a sense of the ambiguity of contemporary life
and the impossibility of grasping reality in the way in which it might
have been possible in the past. In times gone by, human beings could
more or less know all that there was to know. Consequently, Christians lived in a situation in which, precisely because all knowledge
was so accessible, the Church seemed able to comprehend all of it

---

[9] Ibid., 187.

[10] Ibid., 190.

[11] Rahner discusses this critical matter in many places. A very helpful summary of
its meaning and implications can be found in his essay, "The Faith of the Christian
and the Doctrine of the Church," in *Theological Investigations* 14 (New York: Seabury,
1977): 330–56.

within its theological outlook. In those putatively simpler times, the
Christian lived simultaneously within the Christian Church and the
Christian world, at least in principle and, in very many places, in
practice too. "In former times," writes Rahner, "one's task was to
pass from a well-integrated, well-ordered world of knowledge on
to the inconceivable mystery." But today "it is a disordered world
of knowledge which cries out for that light which can only be that
eternal light which does not yet shine upon any man here below."[12]
All human beings, Christians included, struggle with the character
of finite knowledge which is "no longer capable of being reduced to
a complete synthesis" and "which is anti-ideological in character."
Secular knowledge proceeds from sources different from those employed in the official teaching of the Church and "is no longer capable
of being fully synthesized . . . with the message of revelation to us
regarded as an interpretation of this same human life." The modern
Catholic, Rahner adds, "has to recognize and unreservedly endure
this pluralism in his intellectual life, painful and perilous though it
may often seem."[13]

Rahner's point is that life now is much more complex than previously and, consequently, that in determining the appropriate role
of the Church as a historical factor relative to this secular world, we
have to avoid the two tendencies of integrism and esotericism. The
positive relationship of the Church and the secular world cannot be
either the effort to impose the teachings of the Church as a kind of
blueprint or ethical template on the secular world, nor can we simply
withdraw into a negative, entirely critical posture. The history of the
Church/world relationship, argues Rahner, is one of "the Church's
growing self-discovery" and of "the increasing emancipation of the
world into its own secular nature." So we have to guard against
imagining that "all earthly action in the history of the world is nothing but the putting into practice of the principles taught, expounded
and applied by the Church." This attitude, says Rahner, is wrong:

> It is not possible wholly to derive from the principles of natural
> law and the gospel the human action which ought to be done
> here and now, although of course all action must respect those
> principles. Nor when such action is more than the carrying into

[12] Ibid., 335.
[13] Ibid., 356.

effect of those principles and of the official instructions of the Church, does it cease to be morally important from the point of view of God and in relation to him as goal. It still concerns salvation and has to be performed with the absolute earnestness of moral responsibility. It can even be the subject of charismatic inspiration from on high, and, while remaining secular, a factor in the coming of the kingdom of God.[14]

To avoid falling into this trap, thinks Rahner, "the Church herself has a quite new task in relation to this society, a task which might perhaps be characterized as 'prophetic.'"[15] What Rahner does not address, however, is the form of prophecy appropriate to the Church as an institutional actor, and that which is the prerogative of the individual Christian living in the world.

Rahner is committed to the idea that in a democratic society the Church has the right and responsibility to teach and, indeed, to have "a program of action," but, he asks, how is it appropriate for the Church to exercise influence beyond stating principles or the praxis of individual Christians? His answer is not crystal clear. It seems that he sees the Church's role of "instruction" to be prophetic. That is, the teaching on social issues not directly derived from revelation is offered to the world as pastoral/prophetic, as a kind of solemn and serious advice, which, though of course nonbinding on the world, grows out of the Church's concern for the salvation of the world. For this to work, it would be necessary for both individual believers and official representatives of the Church to internalize these prophetic impulses. A whole branch of practical theology, which Rahner rather unhappily named "practical ecclesiological cosmology," needs to be developed precisely to reflect upon the relationship between Church and world at any given time.

In moving toward formulating a practical ecclesiological cosmology for our own times, we can benefit from the recent writings of Archbishop Rowan Williams. In a 2006 address given to the Pontifical Academy of Social Sciences, Rowan Williams, Anglican primate and archbishop of Canterbury, addressed the ambivalence of the Christian Church toward the secular world. Williams identified two forms

[14] Rahner, ed., *Sacramentum Mundi: An Encyclopedia of Theology*, vol. 1 (London: Burns and Oates, 1968), 349–50.
[15] Ibid., 330.

of secularism, which he called "programmatic" and "procedural."
The former is the secularism of "negative" liberty in which the role
of government is to safeguard freedom of choice and eschew the
adoption of any specific moral agenda or particular vision of human
emancipation. The latter is a form of secular society in which "religious convictions are granted a public hearing in debate," though
not necessarily any privilege. Williams sums up the distinction as
one "between the empty public square of a merely instrumental
liberalism, which allows maximal private licence, and a crowded
and argumentative public square which acknowledges the authority
of a legal mediator or broker whose job it is to balance and manage
real difference." Obviously enough, neither the Christian Church
nor other religious bodies can accept a world in which all transcendental values are comprehensively privatized and declared irrelevant
to the formulation of public policies. No calculus of individual and
group benefits, thinks Williams, is possible without addressing "the
question of how society deals with the actual variety and potential
collision of understandings of what is properly human."[16]

While Williams seems largely to agree with Chaput that Christian
insights are important to the health of even a secular, pluralistic society, he seems readier to accept that the Christian voice is simply
one important voice in the public square and that all it can and
should want is to be taken seriously, especially in its commitment
to the transcendent values of human life. Williams would not share
Chaput's conviction that "we are in a struggle for the souls of our
people and our country." Procedural secularity guarantees a level
playing field for the debate between different voices. Certainly, law
may reflect religious or ideological convictions in differing degrees,
depending on the society we are examining and how persuasive
a particular group may have been in promoting one policy or another. In principle, no position is "automatically incapable of being
enshrined in law," says Williams. One can, in principle, win "public
arguments about the need to restrict the availability of abortion"
and one can "win arguments about legalizing euthanasia." And "it
is precisely because such decisions always remain open to argument
that they can be lived with":

<hr>

[16] Rowan Williams, "Secularism, Faith and Freedom" (November 23, 2006),
http://rowanwilliams.archbishopofcanterbury.org/articles.php/1175/rome-lecture
-secularism-faith-and-freedom.

In a society where there were rigidly fixed standards of what could rationally or properly be legislated, there would be the danger of such legal decisions becoming effectively irreformable. It would be harder to reopen questions on the basis of shifting moral perceptions. This is indeed a somewhat high-risk position—but if the alternative is a view that absolutises one and only one sort of public rationality, the risks are higher.[17]

Williams thus rejects both the programmatic secularism that would disqualify religious values from a role in the formation of public policy and any kind of absolutism, ecclesiastical or otherwise, that would enshrine one perspective in secular law (the integrist position). All law in secular society, in other words, is open to revision. It is this, rather than the foolish commitment to negative liberty, that is fundamental to secular liberal democracies.

Here it seems we do encounter a difference of perspective between the public position of many US bishops on the one hand, and Williams on the other. The US bishops have made it quite clear that while there are many serious ethical issues that need to be debated in the public arena, opposition to legalized abortion stands out from all the rest. Catholics may in good conscience, they have argued, dissent from official teaching on, say, the death penalty, but opposition to abortion is a fundamental issue because abortion is itself always wrong. Some critics have tried to argue that a Catholic may hold a pro-life position on abortion and yet be opposed to overturning the federal law that allows abortion (this is a common position for Catholic elected officials). Others have had problems understanding why, according to the bishops, the death penalty is not an equally serious issue and why same-sex marriage apparently is. The fundamental question to be asked about the bishops' position, however, is not about this or that particular item of concern, but the fact that some ethical issues, in their view, leave no room for negotiation.[18] It would certainly be difficult to reconcile this with Williams's position

[17] Ibid.

[18] The bishops themselves do not refer to these teachings as "non-negotiables," as some conservative commentators do, but they are clear that opposition to abortion, euthanasia, embryonic stem-cell research, and same-sex marriage are among the fundamental ethical issues and the pillars of their political vision for American society. See *Forming Consciences for Faithful Citizenship: A Call to Political Responsibility from the Catholic Bishops of the United States*, http://www.usccb.org/faithfulcitizenship?FCStatement.pdf.

and very hard to see how a procedurally secular democracy could entertain a category of values or practices that are a priori not open to discussion. If dialogue is to be possible, it requires a willingness to be persuaded, whereas absolutes evidently foreclose the possibility of serious discussion.[19] Of course, Catholicism, like many other religious traditions, has a set of fundamental religious doctrines that define it and simply cannot be open to change, but these are theological issues with which the public realm is presumably unconcerned. It would be odd, for example, to find the doctrine of the Trinity up for debate between the Church and secular society. Ethical principles (e.g., the fundamental equality in dignity of all human beings or the right to life) are also normative, though unlike theological doctrines they may well need to be explained and justified in the public arena. But dialogue over the reasoning that leads from these principles to particular judgments about their application in society will certainly have to occur, and presumably in principle be open to change, if the word "dialogue" is to mean anything remotely similar to the rest of the world's definition. So, in a procedurally secular society that guarantees a level playing field and admits positions based on convictions about transcendental values, the Church has to be willing to explain why a pro-life stance admits of no exceptions in opposition to abortion, or why opposition to the death penalty is only almost always right, or why the preservation of family life is somehow threatened by same-sex marriage. Not just *that* these are the Church's positions, but *why* they are so. Programmatic secularism will exclude the Church's positions from consideration at all; procedural secularism will welcome them, but the welcome will not mean any special treatment, nor should it. The confidence we have in the rightness of our ethical stands in a pluralistic world should surely be open to testing before the court of public opinion.

A recent book by James Davison Hunter can help us inquire further into how the bishops should or should not act in furthering the

---

[19] Pope Benedict's views on dialogue were more restrictive. At times he saw inter-religious dialogue to be impossible, since the different religions cannot be open to changing their fundamental faith convictions. However, dialogue with philosophy over the nature and possibility of transcendental principles is both possible and necessary. See, for example, Cardinal Ratzinger's 1996 address on "Relativism: The Central Problem for Faith Today," http://www.ewtn.com/library/curia/ratzrela.htm.

presence of the Church in civil society.[20] The problem with Christian efforts to change the world, Hunter argues, is that their approach is utterly wrongheaded and cannot work. They should not be trying to change the world at all. Hunter sums up the "common view of change" as the belief that culture is changed by individual choices. If enough people make the right choices, then, because culture is fundamentally about values, culture will change, possibly dramatically and quickly. On the contrary, says Hunter, culture is neither primarily a product of individual choices nor even of artifacts but rather a creation of networks, elites, technology, and new institutions. The reason, he thinks, that the Christian churches are not a greater force in American culture is because insufficient numbers of their more educated and talented members are prominent in important networks like entertainment, the highbrow press, publishing, the arts, and academia. The vitality of the American churches today, he argues, is in the pew rather than in the leadership, but this means that their energies are peripheral to cultural change. Individuals, even great individuals, do not make change unless they are a part of collectives of like-minded individuals. If we wish to fulfill "the creation mandate" then we have to look to some other means than simply trying to become one political actor among others, trying to motivate the maximum number of individuals to influence the dominant values of the great mass of ordinary people.

Christians fail because they constantly take their understandings of power from those of the dominant strands of the contemporary secular world. Today's world turns to politics and law for solutions to its problems because social consensus is no longer a given. "In short," says Hunter, "the state has become the incarnation of the public weal. . . . My contention is that in response to a thinning consensus of substantive beliefs and dispositions in the larger culture, there has been a turn toward politics as a foundation and structure for social solidarity."[21] Rejecting the negative liberty theory of the modern state as "wrong because it is impossible," he points out that law and policy imply moral judgments and worldviews. And so, "each and every faction in society seeks the patronage of state power as a means of imposing its particular understanding of the

---

[20] James Davison Hunter, *To Change the World: The Irony, Tragedy and Possibility of Christianity in the Late Modern World* (New York: Oxford, 2010).
[21] Ibid., 103.

good on the whole of society."[22] The public becomes conflated with the political; we inflate our expectations of the political process and the will to power comes to dominate our world: "Our times amply demonstrate that it is far easier to force one's will on others through legal and political means or to threaten to do so than it is to persuade them or negotiate compromise with them."[23] People of faith and their institutions are no less affected by this shift than others, since they are concerned about public issues and "as a consequence, faith too has become highly politicized."[24]

Hunter's vision has immediate resonance with the particular situation of the American Roman Catholic Church. There is certainly little doubt that the American episcopate has turned far more than in the past to putting pressure on political society, though whether that has been done in order to impose "its particular understanding of the good on the whole of society" or simply to make space for it within the pluralist consensus is an open question. The United States Conference of Catholic Bishops (USCCB) has made it clear in recent years that it is concerned about particular political initiatives that may seem innocuous but may well have the effect of subtly eroding the religious freedoms central to the American experiment. But what makes it more complicated for the episcopate is that the "thinning consensus of substantive beliefs and dispositions," which Hunter identifies as a mark of the contemporary public space, is also a reality within the Catholic Church itself. While some will see this as a problem of infection, others might simply say that it is a result of the secular space that the Catholic laity in particular inhabit, and that this may have as many positive as negative consequences.[25] It is also possible that Hunter's argument that the absence of moral consequence in society as a whole has led to the state becoming "the incarnation of the public weal" has a parallel within the Church." When Catholics were far less likely to go their own way on ethical issues and more attentive to the voice of Church leaders, there was

---

[22] Ibid., 104.

[23] Ibid., 107.

[24] Ibid., 175.

[25] On this, see Staf Hellemans, "Tracking the New Shape of the Catholic Church in the West," in *Towards a New Catholic Church in Advanced Modernity: Transformations, Visions, Tensions*, ed. Staf Hellemans and Jozef Wissink, Tilburg Theological Studies 5 (Zürich: LIT Verlag, 2012), 19–50.

far less inclination for the bishops to be as vocal or even heavy-handed as they now sometimes seem to be. But when they raise their voices in this way, are they responding to a genuine problem with a sensible solution, or perhaps panicking at the changing face of the American Catholic population?

Hunter considers that problems occur because churches understand themselves as political actors rather than as alternative communities. He imagines a Christian Church in which individuals and their communities of faith engage in "the practice of faithful presence," which "generates relationships and institutions that are fundamentally covenantal in character, the ends of which are the fostering of meaning, purpose, truth, beauty, belonging, and fairness—not just for Christians but for everyone."[26] It is not difficult for a Catholic to see in Hunter's analysis a close parallel to the models of Church as sacrament, as prophet, and as communion. It is, in particular, not hard to find echoes of those haunting opening words of *Gaudium et Spes* that "the joys and hopes, the grief and anguish of the people of our time, especially of those who are poor or afflicted, are the joys and hopes, the grief and anguish of the followers of Christ as well" (GS 1). But it is to Hunter's credit that his vision corrects the Council's tendency to objectify the Church over against the world. The Church shares the lot of modern human beings because the Church is composed of modern human beings, as enmeshed in the concupiscence of the world as they are in the light of Christ. The question for Hunter, however, is whether his vision might not lead to a kind of cultic life in which involvement in the political process becomes less important, not only to the Church as institution, but even to the members of the Church. How do we practice faithful presence as he suggests without abdicating our responsibilities as individual citizens?

If Hunter's depiction of faithful presence is one with which Catholics can identify as at least an ideal of Christian life, though not something we achieve easily or every day, his analysis of the relationship between the public and the political and its connection to power is something that has a lot to teach today's Church. Political change as a means of making the world more Christian is a dead end. Indeed, changing the world is the wrong question because "it makes

---

[26] Hunter, *To Change the World*, 243–48.

the primary subservient to the secondary." The source of the good, God, becomes a tool to achieve the objective of creating "a certain understanding of the good":

> When this happens, righteousness can quickly become cruelty and justice can rapidly turn into injustice. Indeed, history is filled with the bloody consequences of this logic and the logic is very much present, even if implicit, on all sides and in all factions of the ongoing culture war.[27]

There are doubtless many reasons why the American Catholic Church is going through a period of declining influence, some of which are probably beyond its control. The power and unpredictability of the markets, the sweeping cultural changes brought about by globalization and the increasingly pluralistic and secularized character of all but the most isolated states are phenomena that form the given background of the mission and ministry of Christians. It is in this particular world that the Church is called to be a sacrament, not in some bygone world that it imagines it can re-create, nor in some re-Christianized utopia. Christ is the *Lumen Gentium*, the light of the people, and it is the work of the Church to reflect that light upon the world. We might call to mind here the four characteristics of the "social power" of Jesus as Hunter enumerates them: (1) Jesus' power came from submission to the will of God, (2) it rejected status and reputation and privilege, (3) it was characterized by "love for fallen humanity" and for creation, and (4) it was marked by "the non-coercive way in which he dealt with those outside of the community of faith."[28] How are we doing?

The short answer is that our currently deficient theology of the world impedes our capacity to reflect Jesus' social power. Submission to the will of God requires humility and obedience. In the first place, the Church must be humble before the grace of God at work in the world independent of its sacramental status. God's wisdom at work in the world may sometimes act as a corrective to the errors to which the Church as a human institution is prone. If the pagan Cyrus could be the agent of God in restoring the fortunes of Israel, then it is not impossible for the *New York Times* to be part of God's wake-up call to

---

[27] Ibid., 285.
[28] Ibid., 191.

a complacent Church, even if the newspaper's motives might be as nefarious as some of its critics seem to believe. A venal attorney bent on lining his pockets at the Church's expense may still be evidence of the will of God at work. Only arrogance leads the Church automatically to dismiss the wisdom of the world, though of course it need not go to the opposite extreme and bow to any and every whim of the times. The God who moves in mysterious ways is at work in creation, something the Council fathers recognized in their insight that the Church not only teaches the world but also learns from it.[29] And this should also mean that the Church should enter into dialogue with the secular world in the knowledge that divine wisdom may be present in its insights—wisdom that even the Church may not yet have grasped.

The call to reject status and reputation and privilege returns us to Rahner's prophetic Church and to the Church as a "regime of signs," in Alison's phrase. Being able to respond to this challenge will require a much less defensive attitude than we currently tend to favor. Protecting the reputation of the Church may sometimes be an important consideration, but recent events in the Church have shown us that it is most definitely not the highest priority. Becoming defensive happens all too easily when there are internal problems that threaten to become public and damage the Church's public face, as was the case in the failure to respond to many instances of sexual abuse, or when secular authority or public culture treats the Church in a way that seems to its leadership to be demeaning. There is a great deal of disrespect for the Church in our culture today. But for all its secularism, materialism, and ethical indifference, the world retains a lot of respect for Jesus. All of us in the Church need to meditate on that fact. The majority of American Catholics, lay and ordained, are indistinguishable in lifestyle and values from their unchurched fellow citizens, and it is not easy to see how we can witness to countercultural values when we have bought into the opposite.

Love for fallen humanity and for creation brings us to the nub of the issue. It is because we are sinners whom God has forgiven that forgiveness should be in the forefront of our ecclesial posture. Far too many current public pronouncements made in the name of the Church smack of judgmentalism and self-righteousness. We are the Church and there is the world (is the implication), and its salvation

---

[29] See *Gaudium et Spes* 44.

depends on its conforming to our divinely inspired answers to its problems. Of course we mostly do not make the mistake of thinking that the Church knows the best tactics for achieving success on this or that issue of public policy, but far too often we give the impression that *we* have the values that *they* do not, and that we need to impress those values on society. However, love for fallen humanity begins with the awareness that we are among the fallen and that sometimes we may even have fallen somewhat farther than those who do not have the benefit of Christian faith. Whether the Church is right or wrong in its treatment of lesbian and gay Catholics who want their unions to be blessed by the Church, the genuine love that binds them should not simply be dismissed in a subordinate clause of a sentence whose principal point is that their desires are unnatural and their requests impossible to grant. Whether the Church is right or wrong in its claim that all abortions are evil despite the circumstances, prudential judgments of faithful Catholics in agonizing personal circumstances should not be dismissed in a subordinate clause of a sentence whose principal point is that they have excommunicated themselves. Whether the Church is right or wrong that Jesus is the one way to salvation, the sincerity of theologians who struggle with the meaning of this claim for those of other faiths cannot be sidelined in a subordinate clause of a sentence whose principal point is to remove them from their professions and even perhaps their livelihood. There is an appropriate way and an inappropriate way for us to behave as a Christian community; to return to the terminology of James Davison Hunter, the will to power fueled by *ressentiment* is not worthy of our high calling. Or, in Wuerl's words, "The intensity of one's opinion is not the same as the truth. Speaking out of anger does not justify falsehood."[30]

Fourth and finally, Jesus' social power showed itself in the noncoercive way in which he dealt with those outside the community of faith. The heresy of integrism is apparent, however unintentionally, when the Church seeks to impose a Catholic perspective through the ballot box. Of course, the Catholic position on abortion is that it is an objective evil on grounds that do not depend on the Gospel, and therefore that it is binding on all human beings. But even if this is so, it still does not justify efforts to impose this view through the ballot

---

[30] Henneberger, "Wuerl: Why I Won't Deny Pelosi Communion."

box. The way of persuasion is by far the better course of action, not least because it is the more likely to succeed in the long run. The same can be said for every other ethical position the Church holds. Whether or not we believe it to be an ethical absolute, our success in winning its acceptance will depend on the openness of our Church to genuine dialogue and the transparency of the way in which the Church itself lives by the values it wishes society as a whole to adopt.

Where all this leaves us is with a renewed call to become a community of faith that lives by the Gospel, that loves the world in all its concupiscence, and that has the authority to affirm it and to challenge it that comes from the evident effort of the Church to live by the practice of shalom, in faithfulness to Jesus. All Catholics live and work in the world and have the responsibility to be the loving presence of God in all the areas in which they have an influence, but as Hunter reminds us, the Church as an institution will have more impact if it stops trying to change the world, if it abandons its claims, more common among Evangelicals than Catholics, that America was ever really a Christian nation and that through political action it can restore it to that state. There is something to be said for Hunter's view that the best thing the Church can do for now is "to be silent for a season and learn how to enact their faith in public through acts of shalom rather than to try again to represent it publicly through law, policy, and political mobilization."[31] This is not an argument for social quietism. But it is a call for the Church to be the Church.

Objections to the model of the Church/world relationship proposed here might come from more traditional or more liberal perspectives or, indeed, from what Hunter named the neo-Anabaptist school of thought, with which our approach might be confused. To dispense with this last objection first, while the neo-Anabaptist would be attracted to withdrawing the institutional Church from involving itself in the details of the political process, she or he could not accept the love of the world that drives the political dimension of Christian apostolic activity. Nor would the neo-Anabaptists be at all comfortable with the insistence that the baptized Christian is at one and the same time in the Church and the world, and open to the workings of divine grace in both spheres. Liberals would applaud the recognition of the secular dimension of the Christian and

---

[31] Hunter, *To Change the World*, 281.

the turn to the "sinful yet graced" interpretation of secular culture but would be uncomfortable with the danger that this might lead to a lay/clergy split in which the laity were confined to the secular realm as their sphere of activity, leaving the Church once more as a clerical preserve. And the traditionalists would undoubtedly applaud the call for Christians to bring their values to the workaday world but would strongly resist the implication that they do this *ex spiritu* and without the need for a strong teaching authority on matters of politics and civil society.

These objections are met by the following theological principles. First, the Christian Church frees its baptized members to love the world for the sake of the Gospel and to act in the world in the power of the Spirit. Second, the Church structures a believing community gathered around the Eucharist, which is itself a *politeia* given over to the values of the reign of God, but for the sake of the world of which it is inescapably a part. Third, Christians, who are at home in the secular world as they are at home in the Church, find and actualize in the sinful world—as they find and actualize within themselves—the grace of God at work independently of the Church.

Our present ecclesial malaise, then, is a direct result of both overestimating and underestimating the power of the Church. The Church cannot "save the world" but the Church is profoundly important to the health of society. These twin errors could be substantially corrected if we reflected more carefully on the responsibilities entailed in being baptized into the common priesthood of all the faithful. It is this common priesthood, which all—including the ordained—share, which licenses the missionary activity of Christians in the world. In other words, the Church/world relationship is manifest in the activity of the baptized who are at one and the same time secular and religious, at one and the same time sinners and graced. We, all the faithful, are the Church in the world. The Church as visible institution, vis-à-vis the world, is simply one institution among many that make up civil society. The religious meaning of this Church lies in the support it gives to the mission of the baptized, graced and sinful in a graced and sinful world, above all through the liturgy. In the liturgy of word and sacrament the Church supports the faith of Christians in the saving work of Christ, and everything else it does of value is secondary to this purpose. The Church reflects the light of Christ onto the world when the world sees the faith-filled humanity of countless Christians, grace-filled and sinners like themselves.

We are in danger of radically misconceiving our responsibilities to the work of the Church in the world when we, as a Church, insert ourselves into political controversy. The temptation to overreach ourselves and lean toward the integrism against which Rahner warned and which is an ever-present temptation for the Church when it faces what it takes to be an antagonistic world is not wrong solely because it falsely assumes that the world needs a Christian template laid upon it to replace worldly error with inspired truth. It is also wrong because such a vision can only be implemented if baptized Christians are thought of as so many foot soldiers in a salvation strategy devised by High Command. Baptism does not make some of us foot soldiers and others commissioned officers. It includes us all in a priestly people, called to be prophetic (to teach the world) and to be "kingly" (to serve the world). The Church is there to aid us in this task that baptism has brought upon us, and we would be foolish to ignore the support it has to offer and the instruction that it has to give. But in the last analysis we act in the world through the power of the Holy Spirit who guides us, in the light of our conscience, knowing full well the dangers of our sinfulness and the power of grace.

This position would undoubtedly seem to some to seriously undercut traditional notions of authority in the Catholic Church. While they would certainly accept that the whole people of God is "priestly" in the sense described above, what of the identification of ordained ministry, especially that of the bishop, with "teaching, ruling and sanctifying"? Proclaiming the Church "essentially an unequal society," Pius X famously added that "the one duty of the multitude is to allow themselves to be led and, like a docile flock, to follow the Pastors."[32] And if it would be rare today to find someone echoing the pope's words exactly, there is much in the kind of pastoral practice we have discussed above that seems not too far from this understanding of the lay/clergy relationship. But the role of Church leadership in matters of civil society not directly connected to revealed truth is one of guidance of the community of faith (Rahner calls it "instruction"), not one of partisan engagement in the political process, nor one of harsh judgments on specific individuals who are adjudged to be at variance from some particular teaching.

---

[32] Pope Pius X, *Vehementer Nos*, 8.

That a baptized Christian acts in the world in his or her apostolic, missionary role in virtue of baptism, and not by direct commission of the institutional Church, is well attested in the tradition. One of the longer treatments of this complex point is to be found in Yves Congar's efforts to explain the relationship between the ministry of the individual Christian *ex spiritu* and the formally mandated organizations of Catholic Action. While his purpose is to confirm the benefits of Catholic Action, he insists that it would be wrong "to forget that it is the organization of an already living apostleship, one grounded in the deepest realities of Christian life." "In this context," writes Congar, "every faithful Christian can and ought to adopt the magnificent saying of John Wesley, 'I look upon all the world as my parish.'"[33] So if the Church is at work in the world in and through the apostolic activity of all the faithful, including the laity, the nature of the individual's relationship to ecclesiastical authority depends on what is at issue. Individual Christians have no role in formulating basic doctrines or proclaiming fundamental ethical principles, though they can surely try to reexpress them in ways their fellow citizens might grasp. But they have the starring roles in the evangelical drama of simply being the face of Christ in culture and civil society—a task that means that every day, in all that they do, they are willy-nilly interpreting Christian faith in a secular world. This is only possible in the power of the Spirit.

When the energies of American Church leadership are not being devoted to damage control because of financial irregularities or, more commonly, the continuing tragedy of sex abuse, they seem to be disproportionately expended on campaigning in the political world on a variety of issues and not sufficiently taken up with strengthening the life of faith of the community. We do not have a strong Church when we have vociferous "church patriotism" working to exercise "crystallized group violence" in the name of the Church as a "system of goodness." We have a strong Church when the life of prayer and sacraments enables a sinful people to engage constructively with the concupiscence of the world of which we are a part. We have a strong Church when we show in our manner of proceeding that our convictions and commitments make for a more compassionate community filled with a concern for human flourishing out of love for God. We

---

[33] Congar, *Lay People in the Church*, 366.

do not have a strong Church when we are expending energy on laying burdens on people unnecessarily, or when we are conspicuously
preferring the letter of the law to the spirit of the Gospel. We have a
strong Church when we see it as a community of faith, and a weak
Church when we confuse the institutional structures with the life
of faith. They are there to enable, they are not "it."

The practical implications of such a view of the Church change
the way in which the Church acts in the world. It is of course important for the Church to proclaim doctrine, to teach firmly on ethical
principles, and to suggest ways in which these doctrines might be
defended and these principles might be furthered. But the Church
is present in the world as teacher primarily in and through the prophetic activity of the priestly people. Solidarity with victims, compassion for the suffering, and identification with our fellow human
beings in the ambiguity of our tasks as sinners who are yet graced
by God are reflections of the light of Christ where the enunciation of
law is not. We are present in the world as teachers when we embrace
the ambiguity of our concupiscent world as it struggles haltingly, but
with the grace of God, to move beyond its own sinfulness to embrace
the "other" as a child of God, whether a slave or sweatshop worker,
a gay man or lesbian, an alien, or even a "mere" woman. God will
find the answers through our apostolic activity in the world; they
are not already there in some institutional formulae. The apostle is
sent by God, by means of the Church; the true meaning of Church
is "the body of those called together in communion and sent by God
into the world." Everything else ecclesial is secondary.

Among the implications of all the above is that the role of bishops
in the Church is both more important and less important than seems
to be the current perception. Their role is more important as the
spiritual guides that *Lumen Gentium* understood them to be, especially
if we understand the role of the Church to be that of a "peaceable
community" of Gospel values, in other words, as a sacrament, as the
leaven in the mass or the salt that gives savor. If this responsibility
to teach and, yes, to govern is exercised as the Council documents
intend, then all the faithful will be the better able to exercise their
baptismal priesthood in the wider secular world of which we are all a
part. This will happen as informed and compassionate citizens, not as
a pressure group. The bishops' role is less important in the sense that
they do not govern as political actors and they are not responsible
for lobbying for political change. The Church itself is not a lobbying

organization. But guided in the principles of the Gospel, citizens can act out their baptismal responsibilities to change the world. If we really were the effective peaceable community that we ought to be, and not the dysfunctional crisis-ridden and scandal-struck institution that we are in the popular imagination, then think how much influence we might have. And how solemn and sacred would be the awesome responsibility of our bishops to inform and inspire us, to exercise their episcopal power—that is, to empower all the faithful.

PART 2

The Ministry of the Laity

□ □ □

Is Baptism enough? Is it sufficient for evangelization? Or do
we rather "hope" that the priest should speak, that the bishop
might speak . . . and what of us? Then, the grace of baptism
is somewhat closed, and we are locked in our thoughts, in our
concerns. Or sometimes think: "No, we are Christians, I was
baptized, I made Confirmation, First Communion . . . I have
my identity card all right. And now, go to sleep quietly, you are
a Christian. But where is this power of the Spirit that carries
us forward?" When we do this, the Church becomes a mother
church that produces children [and more] children, because
we, the children of the Church, we carry that. But when we
do not, the Church is not the mother but the babysitter that
takes care of the baby—to put the baby to sleep. It is a Church
dormant. Let us reflect on our Baptism, on the responsibility
of our Baptism.

—Pope Francis's homily, Casa Santa Marta,
April 17, 2013

Chapter 4

The Laity in *Lumen Gentium*

One of the finest accomplishments of *Lumen Gentium* is that it resituates the lay person at the center of Christian life. Although there have been great lay Christians throughout the history of the Church, overwhelmingly the Church's sense of itself has been marked by amnesia about the 95 percent of the community of faith who are *not* ordained and *not* vowed religious. Beginning perhaps with Jesus of Nazareth, the lay person who stands at the origin of the Christian Church, the status of being "lay" has largely been of little interest to Christian theology. Ordination, hierarchy, monasticism, sacramental ministry, structures of authority and canon law, and doctrinal and moral teaching have all rightly been the object of intense theological reflection. But the fundamental building block of the Church—the believing Christian—is largely taken for granted in the history of theology. Until, that is, the Second Vatican Council turned its attention to lay people.

Although Vatican II produced an entire decree titled The Apostolic Activity of Lay People, in which it had much of interest to say about what lay people *do* in the Church and outside it, our principal concern will be the treatment of lay people in *Lumen Gentium*, where the focus is a little more—though insufficiently—on who they *are* rather than simply what they *do*. If indeed it is true, as the Council has said, that the baptismal and ordained priesthoods are different in essence, though related to one another, then it cannot be the case that either priesthood is distinguished from the other simply because of the work that lay people or clergy are called to. The still-prevailing "character theology" of priesthood presents ordination as placing an indelible mark upon the soul of the ordained, through which he is ontologically changed.[1] And, in baptism, the sacrament of initiation that admits new Christians into the Church, we become "a new creation," which surely implies, if it does not actually state, a similar ontological claim. In both cases, the two sacraments are understood to make us into different beings than we were before we received them. A passive Christian is no less baptized than Catherine of Siena, and a lazy priest is no less ordained than the Curé of Ars.

A perceptive reader may at this point protest that baptism is not the mark of the lay person but that of the Christian, and he or she would be absolutely correct, for the ordained minister is as surely baptized as the lay person and probably spent many years as a baptized lay person before the ceremony of ordination. However, while the newly ordained priest retains the baptismal priesthood while entering the hierarchical priesthood, he is no longer a lay person. Not only does this prove the truth of the claim that baptism is not the mark of the lay person, but it also shows very clearly that, sacramentally speaking, there is no mark of the lay status that lay people possess and ordained ministers do not. Herein lies the problem of defining what it is to be a lay person. It is quite easy to define what it is to be a Christian—a baptized believer—and equally unproblem- atic to identify a priest as one who has received the sacrament of orders. But while the ordained minister, again according to current rather traditional understandings is ontologically distinguished from the lay person, the lay person can be understood ontologically only as a baptized Christian (like the priest) who has not received the sacrament of orders. It is this set of observations that lies behind Yves Congar's observation that the Church has tended to treat lay people as "negative creatures"—that is, as neither ordained nor as vowed religious.

As we shall shortly see, the Council fathers recognized the com- plexity of this set of problems by ignoring the question of the onto- logical status of the lay person. Whether this represents some of the unfinished business of the Council or simply a wise decision to await a moment when history reveals an urgency to address the problem anew remains to be seen. But while they did not take this particular

---

[1] On this, see Vatican II's Decree on the Ministry and Life of Priests, *Presbyterorum Ordinis*, 2.

bull by the horns, they nevertheless had much to say about this great moment for the vast majority of baptized Christians, those perceived to be "just" the laity.

What Is a Lay Person in *Lumen Gentium*?

Much has been made of the struggles of the Council fathers at the second session in 1963 over how to structure *Lumen Gentium*. One of the more momentous and telling of their decisions was to divide the material they had at one time gathered into a chapter on the laity into two parts. After an initial chapter expounding the biblical images for the Church and exploring its relationship to Christ, the bishops decided to place the first part of that material in a chapter on "the People of God" to precede chapter 3 on the hierarchical nature of the Church. The second half of the material, on the laity, would follow the chapter on hierarchy. We can never overestimate the importance of the decision to make chapter 2 an exploration of the baptismal priesthood of the people of God. It is Christ who "made the new people 'a kingdom of priests to his God and Father'" (10). This priestly people "shares also in Christ's prophetic office," which in practical terms means that all the baptized share a teaching role in the world, and all are called to holiness and blessed with spiritual gifts (12). On the other hand, it is also significant, though less frequently noticed, that turning to the hierarchy before discussing the laity is a reversion to a pyramidal understanding of the Church that is by no means implied in a proper understanding of hierarchy. Of course, the consequences of keeping together the material contained in the current chapters 2 and 4 and placing all of it before a discussion of hierarchy would have been even more revolutionary. It would suggest, among other things, that hierarchy is an element within a baptismal understanding of the whole priestly community. As things stand in the document, it reinforces a different vision, in which the rooting of hierarchy in apostolic authority cannot but make us see lay people as subordinate if not second-class members of the community of faith.

Chapter 4, titled "The Laity," begins with a reference back to chapter 2 with the strong assertion that "everything that has been said of the people of God is addressed equally to laity, religious and clergy" (30). There then follows the clarification that "laity" is taken to mean everyone except clergy and those in religious life:

That is, who by Baptism are incorporated into Christ, are constituted the People of God, who have been made sharers in their
own way in the priestly, prophetic and kingly office of Christ and
play their part in carrying out the mission of the whole christian
people in the church and in the world. (31)

While this is helpful as a rubric it is certainly questionable as a judgment. The problem with such a distinction, as many a religious sister
has had occasion to notice, is that it places religious life in an inter-
mediary category between laity and clergy and in practice leads to
its inclusion as "quasi-clerical" or "lay" as the occasion suits. Since
religious qua religious are not ordained and religious sisters cannot
at the present time be ordained, and since their religious profession
does not offer them an "ontological change" parallel to that in baptism or holy orders, it would seem that theologically they should be
classified as lay people, regardless of canon law.

The probable reason for the exclusion of vowed religious from the
ranks of the laity lies in the definition of the laity as pursuing Christian mission "in the world," and this is not without its problems. As
the fathers comment, "To be secular is the special characteristic of
the laity," and this is the closest the Council ever came to an essential or ontological claim about the lay state. However, the remaining sentences in section 31, immediately following the statement of
the secular character of the laity, complicate the matter, stating that
"people in holy Orders may sometimes be engaged in secular activities" and that religious "bear outstanding and striking witness that the
world cannot be transfigured and offered to God without the spirit of
the beatitudes." So much for the special characteristic of the laity. If this
is not saying that while clergy can sometimes do the work of the laity,
the opposite is never true, then it is perhaps the recognition that the
simple distinctions employed here do not do justice to the complexity
of the world. Indeed, the definition of laity quoted above clearly says
that the laity engage in mission "in the Church and in the world." A
description of the respective responsibilities of clergy, religious, and
laity that ignored ontological issues would look something like this:
"The work of lay people is primarily in the secular world, and so is that
of many vowed religious, and while the clergy have particular leadership responsibilities in the internal life of the community of faith, most
of them live in the world too." (The only exception here just might
be enclosed communities of male and female religious, who separate

themselves from the world, though not from its concerns.) Since the term "secularity" is evidently not used of the laity to mean that they are somehow divorced from their Christian life and its responsibilities, one could just as easily maintain that clergy and religious are secular too, and, indeed, that the Church itself is a secular reality.[2]

Once they step away from complexities incurred through the specter of ontological change, the bishops are on much firmer ground as they go on to describe the way in which lay mission is typically exercised, though it still leaves an important question unanswered. The laity live in the world and contribute to its sanctification "from within, like leaven . . . by fulfilling their own particular duties." The witness of their lives is instrumental in illuminating the temporal order. This is both true and significant, indeed far more significant than perhaps we notice. For if the Church is indeed "the leaven in the mass" or the salt that gives savor to the food, its mission seems then to be equated with lay mission. So if the work of the Church is hidden in the humble human goodness of ordinary people, there are two obvious questions. First, how should we evaluate the charitable works of religious sisters who, over the centuries, have run schools, hospitals, orphanages, and other institutions? And second, how exactly do ordained ministers contribute to the sanctification of the world? The first question is easily answered by asserting that religious sisters are indeed more like laity than clergy and their work has primarily been in the secular world. The second question eludes easy answers. As baptized Christians, the clergy share the lay responsibility for the edification of the secular world. The something extra that is incurred in sacramental ordination, however, places them simultaneously in a more visible position in the Church as a public sign of the values of the Gospel and in a less significant position in terms of direct evangelization. *Lumen Gentium* is clear that the laity "have as brothers those who have been placed in the sacred ministry and who by Christ's authority, through teaching, sanctifying and ruling so nourish the family of God that the new commandment of love may be fulfilled by all" (32). The role of the ordained ministers, in other words, is to be enablers in the work of evangelization broadly construed. Their role is more public, their influence on the world

[2] On this, see Paul Lakeland, *The Liberation of the Laity: In Search of an Accountable Church* (New York: Continuum, 2003), 149–85.

less direct. They are doing their work not so much as the leaven in the mass but more as "the lamp on the lampstand, giving light to the whole world." But the light only truly reflects the light of Christ on the world to the degree that the laity, the vanguard of evangelization, are inspiring it through the example of holy living. Writing about the destiny of the world as one "in justice, in love and in peace," the Council fathers insist that "the laity enjoy a principal role in the universal fulfillment of this task" (36).

If it is true that the essentially secular role of the laity, correctly understood, places them in the forefront of the mission of the Church to the world and leads to understanding the role of (ordained) Church leaders as enablers, then it is important to recognize that this lay role—though enabled by leadership—is not delegated by anyone other than Christ himself. When the bishops reiterate that "the apostolate of the laity is a sharing in the church's saving mission," they immediately qualify their statement: "Through Baptism and Confirmation all are appointed to this apostolate by the Lord himself." The mission, which is proper and peculiar to the laity, "to make the church present and fruitful in those places and circumstances where it is only through them that it can become the salt of the earth" (33) is something that each lay person carries out on the authority of Christ, given in the sacraments of baptism and confirmation. The bishop or the pastor has no say in this, though he obviously has enormous responsibility as an enabler, since the quality of lay presence in the world is at least partially dependent on the quality of the catechesis they have received. Essentially, secular lay ministry is not just living in the world as a good person, but living in the world in the light of the Gospel. Perhaps the awesome responsibility of leadership was what gave St. Augustine sleepless nights: "When I am frightened by what I am to you, then I am consoled by what I am with you. To you I am the bishop, with you I am a Christian. The first is an office, the second a grace; the first a danger, the second salvation."[3]

The complexity of the relations of clergy, religious, and laity is further indicated by the text's observation that in addition to this apostolate carried out in virtue of baptism, "the laity can be called in different ways to more immediate cooperation in the apostolate

---

[3] St. Augustine, Sermon 340, 1. Quoted in LG 32.

of the hierarchy" (33). The language of "cooperation in hierarchical ministry" is a clear sign that the bishops are thinking of what was then called Catholic Action. Indeed, they refer to an allocution of Pius XII, who with his immediate predecessor was a major proponent of this idea that lay people could be organized into officially recognized apostolic associations.[4] By the time of the Council, however, the heyday of Catholic Action was over, though it continued for a time especially in Latin countries, and its spirit is still alive in organizations like the Knights of Columbus and even in the lay divisions of movements like Opus Dei and the Legionaries of Christ. But perhaps the bishops were somehow aware of the new world that was impending, as they added of lay people that "they have, moreover, the capacity of being appointed by the hierarchy to some ecclesiastical offices with a view to a spiritual end," and so the way was made "clear for them to share diligently in the salvific work of the Church according to their ability and the needs of the times" (33). In our times, half a century after the Council, more and more of the work of the Church itself is being taken up by one or other form of lay ministry, commissioned or otherwise. It may be that one of the most important pieces of unfinished business is the clarification of the relationship between the work of ordained ministers and that of lay people. The degree to which lay ecclesial ministry has developed in the US Church in particular raises the question whether this work is the appropriate exercise of baptismal priesthood or, in the phrase I wish I had invented but did not, simply, "the apostolate of the second string." Is this the proper work of the laity, or are they bench players or reserves who have been called upon in an emergency that the team coach fondly hopes is temporary?

Cooperation in Mission and Ministry

In their work of bringing the light of Christ to the world, the laity must cooperate with one another, says *Lumen Gentium*, so that by working together, they can bring the world closer to "the rules of justice" and "the practice of virtue," through which it "is better prepared for the seed of the divine word." They have to walk a tightrope between their responsibilities as members of the Church and those

---

[4] *Six ans sont écoulé* (October 5, 1957): AAS 49 (1957), p. 927.

of the secular world, "which is governed by its own principles," and be especially careful to resist the erosion of freedom of religion (36). Lay people do all this by exercising their baptismal responsibilities in the world without the direct intervention of the Church, though of course in the light of its teaching. Today, perhaps more so than at the time of the Council, Catholic lay people active in ministry are likely to be better educated, especially in theology and Scripture. Because this means that they need to refer to the assistance of the clergy less frequently than in the past, it raises in acute form the issue that the Council fathers next went on to discuss: the fraternal and pastoral relationship of the clergy, especially the local pastor, and the community of faith that he leads.

Section 37, which closes the chapter on the laity, examines in detail the way in which the ordained ministers and lay people should interact and it rewards close attention. It begins by asserting the rights of the laity to the help of their clergy, "especially that of the word of God and the sacraments." Immediately, this is qualified with the statement beloved of today's Catholic reform movements that "to the extent of their knowledge, competence or authority the laity are entitled, and indeed sometimes duty-bound, to express their opinion on matters which concern the good of the church." If and when this proves necessary, the text continues in words not so beloved of these same reform movements, "this should be done through the institutions established by the church for that purpose." These actions of the laity should be marked by truth, courage, prudence, reverence, and charity. While "the laity should promptly accept in christian obedience what is decided by the pastors," the pastors in their turn "should recognize and promote the dignity and responsibility of the laity" and "willingly use their prudent advice and confidently assign offices to them in the service of the church, leaving them freedom and scope for activity." There is a clear indication by the bishops that fostering this kind of relationship between the pastor and the people is a benefit to both. Lay responsibility is strengthened and their enthusiasm for cooperation is enhanced, while the pastors in their turn "are enabled to judge more clearly and more appropriately in spiritual and in temporal matters."

The clear message of this discussion is that there is a separation of function between the pastors and the laity, but in a common cause, and their respective responsibilities are exercised in an atmosphere of mutual respect. For all its merits, however, there is one discordant note and one gaping hole in the argument. A careful reading of the four paragraphs that this section is divided into reveals that all the points are made quite well in the first, third, and fourth. With everything that is said about lay responsibility, there is also the appropriate stress on "reverence and charity towards those, who, by reason of their office, represent the person of Christ." Paragraph 2, however, is one of those periodic reaffirmations of truth in traditional language and with an unnecessarily heavy-handed style. It is not wrong, just out of place:

> Like all the faithful, the laity should promptly accept in christian obedience what is decided by the pastors who, as teachers and rulers of the church, represent Christ. In this they will follow Christ's example who, by his obedience to the point of death, opened the blessed way of the liberty of the children of God to all of humanity. (37)

The following paragraphs reassert the more even-handed and pastoral tone of the entire section, leading to the suspicion that, once again, the need to satisfy those of a more traditional disposition explains the unnecessary stress on obedience. Obedience, as a Christlike response to the teaching authority of the Church on matters of doctrinal moment, is one thing but to invoke Christ's example in order to insist on a quiescent attitude in face of the local pastor's prudential decisions is entirely another and does not fit at all well with the recognition both of the lay persons' right and responsibility to be assertive when necessary and of the pastor's needs at times to be guided by their good sense and expertise.

The second concern, the "gaping hole" we have to address occurs in the context of the refreshing and important insistence on the right and responsibility of the lay person to speak her or his mind "on those things which pertain to the good of the Church." For an example of what might be such an occasion we need look no further, of course, than the responsibility of the laity to speak out on the issue of clerical sexual abuse of minors. One of the reasons why so much abuse in the time of the Council and before was not made public was because of the collusion of bishops and pastors in hiding it. The other was the timidity of the laity, a phenomenon only encouraged by their pastors. But an additional reason why the laity were so often silent on such a serious matter was that there simply were and largely still are no appropriate institutional vehicles for speaking out. The laity should speak out, when necessary, "through the institutions established by the Church for that purpose," says the document. But what precisely are those institutions? Where in our current ecclesial life is there an institution through which laity may appropriately have voice? These "institutions" simply do not exist and when laity give voice to their concerns in noninstitutional venues, it then becomes so easy to classify them as "dissidents." The evident message of the Council fathers is that there will be times when serious issues will lead lay people to take stands for the good of the Church that will be critical of prevailing practice or past or present abuses. How to exercise this right and responsibility remains a serious challenge for responsible lay people today, and one that *Lumen Gentium* failed to address or perhaps left to the developing wisdom of the Church of the future.

Laity, Clergy, and the Good of the Church

For all the remarkable insights and fundamental shifts in orientation that the treatment of the laity in *Lumen Gentium* represents, the decision to see them simply in distinction from their ordained ministers is a serious flaw, contributing greatly to much of the disquiet in today's Church in Europe and North America. Because the bishops were either unable or unwilling to tackle the question of the theological status of the laity, they fell back on the important but secondary question of role differentiation between lay people and ordained ministers. However, the clergy continue to be seen as somehow ontologically changed by their ordination, while the laity are discussed as baptized Christians *tout court*. Through the power of orders the clergy are changed, though in such a way that they do not lose their status as members of the baptismal priesthood but have ministerial priesthood added on. They are changed and yet not changed. They are changed through ordination and this brings responsibilities of leadership, but the Council document is at great pains to stress the radical equality of all Christians in virtue of their common baptism and their common responsibility for the evangelization of the world.

This question of the theological relationship between laity and clergy was a major concern of Yves Congar, OP, one of the greatest influences on the Council, who in the early 1960s was rethinking a number of positions he had taken in his great book, *Lay People in the*

Church,[5] published a decade earlier. When he issued a second edition,[6] he took as his starting point the idea of the people of God, just then being introduced into *Lumen Gentium*. The "hierarchical fact," he says, "is set within this whole People of God." But this does not mean that the mission itself is divided into parts. Rather, "there are particular forms of the exercise of the Church's mission, but there is no particular mission differentiating the faithful and the ministerial priesthood." A "classification of the layman by reference to the cleric" was no longer acceptable.[7] Indeed he wrote several years later that, since the Council, "it is no longer the layman who stands in need of definition but the priest."[8] It is fair to say that this discussion remains to be completed; if baptism is what makes a Christian, then what is the extra something a priest acquires that does not make the idea of a lay person somehow a kind of remainder concept, even a remainder who are more than 95 percent of the whole? The designation of the lay person as "secular" raises more questions than it solves.

The laity and the ordained priesthood are evidently intended to collaborate for the good of the world, and this may be where the misunderstandings arise. In the centuries between the Council of Trent and Vatican II, the good of the world was not a particular concern of the Church. Rather, the Church was concerned with the good of God's Church, understood in distinction from and often antagonistic toward the world. When the focus is on the internal realities of the Church, especially when it is on the defensive, there are obvious reasons why the roles of the clergy are primarily those of spiritual and pastoral leadership and those of the laity involve principally faithfulness to the sacraments and obedience to the voice of ministerial authority. It is also not irrelevant that this period of time coincided with one in which the laity had neither the education nor the inclination to challenge the wisdom, if not the authority, of ecclesial teaching.

When Vatican II began to reflect directly on the Church it saw it primarily as an evangelical reality. *Lumen Gentium* opens with the

---

[5] Originally published as *Jalons pour une théologie du laicat* (Cerf, 1954; English trans. Newman Press, 1965).

[6] In 1964; English trans., 1967.

[7] Congar, *Laypeople in the Church: A Study for a Theology of Laity*, 2nd edition (Long Prairie, MN: Newman Press, 1965), 25.

[8] Congar, "My Pathfindings in the Theology of Laity and Ministries," *The Jurist* 2 (1972): 181–82.

statement that "Christ is the light of the nations" and this light "is resplendent on the face of the Church." The Council "ardently desires to bring all humanity that light of Christ . . . by proclaiming his Gospel to every creature" (1). Any consideration of internal issues in the Church was governed by the sense that the Church exists as a sacrament of the love of God in the world, as the leaven in the mass, the salt that gives savor to the food, or the lamp that shines for the light of Christ on the world. A faithful Church is one that is oriented to mission, therefore, and once the Council makes that axial shift, the whole question of lay and clerical cooperation becomes much more complicated, since the baptismal priesthood and not ministerial authority is the warrant for the evangelical role or apostolate of the laity. The much-examined struggle or conflict between a more traditional minority of the Council fathers and a larger number of more pastorally oriented bishops is in part about the degree of emphasis that should be given to internal concerns and the extent to which mission should drive the conciliar agenda. The more the focus remains on internal issues, the more likely it is that traditional categories will remain unquestioned. The more attention is given to evangelization broadly understood, the more stress these traditional categories undergo. Both internal and external orientations are present in the Council documents, but the weight of the great constitutions *Lumen Gentium* and *Gaudium et Spes* clearly indicates that at the time of the Council, at least the opening to the world had priority.

Looking at the challenges that face the Church today, it is evident that the agenda of mission continues to be significant, but the means that the Council fathers seemed to envisage would be utilized to realize it have undergone some rethinking, at least in the minds of Church leadership. It is as if the leaders of the Church desire to continue its outreach to the world as eagerly as did Vatican II, but without allowing the traditional categories of clergy and laity to develop and change in response to the different conditions that now prevail. It is, for example, even more the responsibility of the laity to be the Christian presence in the world when the clergy are declining so rapidly in numbers. And yet the papacies of John Paul II and especially that of Benedict XVI have shown a determination to shore up the traditional patterns of priesthood and to recentralize authority in the person of the pope at just the time at which, perhaps, an educated laity at home in the world should be given some credit for knowing how to be mature and accountable Christians. Moreover, this same crisis in the priesthood has meant that many of the most pastorally active lay people have been drawn into ministries formerly restricted to clergy and religious. And finally, those apostolic associations of lay people that are active in today's world, where they are not purely charitable, largely present a Church that is not at all at home in the world but rather in the same defensive or even antagonistic posture toward it that the Council tried so hard to overcome.

The challenging questions with which we are left about the character and forms of ministry in the Church, the meaning of "the lay vocation" and the responsibility that lay people have for being in the front line of dialogue with the world, and the kind of leadership that the hierarchical priesthood ought to be providing to the ranks of the baptismal priesthood stem in large part from the unanswered questions of *Lumen Gentium*. Whether it was a wise tactical decision or a failure of nerve, the absence of a clear theological reflection on the laity left much work to be done. The difficult relationships between the laity and at least the higher ranks of the clergy in North America and Europe at the present time testify to the fact that the fine words of *Lumen Gentium* about cooperation between the two "orders" may just not be sufficient. And so we turn now to a more detailed discussion of the issues raised by the idea of "vocation," and in particular that of the vocation of the laity.

Chapter 5

Vocation in the Church

It has not at all been the practice in the Catholic Church to talk as if there is one single vocation of all the baptized. For very many years the Catholic Church has used the term vocation almost exclusively to refer to ordained ministry and to religious life. There is a vocation to priesthood, to the diaconate, and to orders of men and women in what has also been called "consecrated life." That has left everyone else with no vocation. The young man who entered the seminary and departed after a couple of years might say, on reflection, "I thought I had a vocation but I didn't." The former novice nun, likewise. And we all know what "let us pray for more vocations" means in most Church circles.

The churches of the Protestant Reformation rejected the idea that "vocation" was a term reserved to priesthood and religious life (and, indeed, largely rejected the idea of religious life altogether). In making this break, they admitted lay people to the ranks of those with a calling, but they also greatly expanded the number of "vocations" so that, in the end, vocation came to be understood to be the job or profession one had, especially if it was lived out faithfully in the context of a Christian life. God had called a person to be a teacher or a carpenter, and it was one's Christian duty to be the best possible teacher or carpenter. And while the idea of doing one's best has some Christian spiritual potential, over time it often came to mean that simply doing one's job meant responding to God's call and that was the end of that.

We have been considerably wrongheaded, Catholic and Protestant alike, in our use of the idea of vocation or calling, but in what follows we will concentrate on the Catholic Church and the Catholic "crisis of vocations." It is axiomatic that "crisis of vocations" includes but is by no means exhausted by the fact of a shortage of ordained ministers. As a matter of fact, both Catholics and Protestants have something to teach the other, while both suffer from a similar deficiency. The Catholic tradition in its focus on ordination or religious vows has preserved the sense that a vocation is somehow something considerably more than the job one does, but at the price of abandoning 95 percent of the baptized to the ranks of those who "do not have a vocation." Protestantism overcame that problem and has much to teach Catholics in that regard, but it also removed the sense that we are called to something above and beyond the work we do. The plumber and the pope are surely called to something more than just being a plumber or being a pope.

My underlying assumption in this chapter is that the natural, almost instinctive understanding of Catholics that the Church is composed of clergy and laity is deeply unhelpful and, if not actually theologically dubious, arguably socially and structurally harmful.

The word "church" is an unhappy choice of word to translate the Greek *ekklesia*, at least if we wish to have any good sense of the original meaning of the term. The *ekklesia* is the gathering of any group for some public purpose. The word refers to the condition of being gathered together and to the gathered community. It translates very happily into the Latin *congregatio* and hence into the English "congregation." Behind the word *ekklesia* lies the notion of "being called out" of some larger group in order to form this smaller public group with a definite purpose. The members of the *ekklesia*, the *ekkletoi*, are those called out and called together. The Christian *ekklesia* is then all those called out and called together by Jesus Christ to the glory of God and gathered together for worship.

It is evident that the fundamental meaning of *ekklesia* is of a single calling together in God's service, in which itself there is no sense of hierarchy, priority, or ordering in ranks. In this respect, the word functions exactly as the Greek word *laos* or "people" in the phrase, actually not particularly common in the Hebrew Bible, the *laos tou theou*, or "people of God." In fact, the word *ekklesia* is also sometimes used in the New Testament in the phrase *ekklesia tou theou*, thus implying in its specificity that there are other kinds of gatherings for quite other purposes. The development of the term *laos* from its original meaning as the whole people to the point where it designates those who have no particular office within the Church is contested, especially the length of time that it took to get to the point of singling out the clergy from the laity. Pretty much everyone will agree, however, that the earliest meaning of the term, in both the Hebrew Scriptures and the New Testament, is simply that of one people or even of a large group of people.

In *Lumen Gentium* we can see how particular and deliberate is the clear preference in this document for the image of "People of God" (*laos tou theou*) to describe the Church (*ekklesia tou theou*). The choice of this phrase is not arbitrary. It is a quite deliberate effort on the part of the Council fathers to say that "before we are many, we are one," symbolized, of course, in placing the chapter on people of God before the chapter on the hierarchical nature of the Church. There are certainly some interpreters of the Council, especially those who would like to "reform the reform," as they say, who consider the image of communion to be more central than that of people of God. But communion, though certainly important, seems to mean "though we are many we are one," and that is not quite the same thing.

If the *ekklesia* or *congregatio* are those called out and gathered together for a particular purpose, what exactly is the purpose? What is the purpose implied in the modifier "*tou theou*"? What does it mean to be called out and gathered together for God's purpose? The first thing to establish is that it surely cannot be just the gathering together that exhausts the purpose. If that were all it was, it would be like being issued with the team uniform but then left to stand around wondering if there was a game to be played. Yes, we are a team, but what are we a team for? What is the game we are involved in because we are on God's team? If we are simply "waiting for Godot," then we have somehow missed the point.

For much of its history the Church has treated the team precisely as if it were "waiting for Godot," though it has been asked to pass the time in a whole variety of exercises and duties, no doubt to stave off the dullness of merely waiting. Baptism was the moment when we received the uniform (symbolized today still by the white garment given to the newly baptized) as a sign that we had joined the *ekklesia tou theou*, God's team. But the responsibilities that followed from baptism were internal to the team. We had to keep the uniform clean, be kind to our teammates, obey the coach, and thank, praise, and bless God for admitting us to the team. Since we didn't or couldn't succeed in not besmirching the uniform, we had to do penance in order to get it clean again. We did all this sitting around, keeping clean and doing penance for a lifetime, and with luck our salvation was secure. But almost all ministry was in the hands of the clergy, and the rest of us didn't actually have to do anything, though there were a lot of things that we had not to do.

The passivity of the lay life—symbolized in its not being considered to be a particular calling or vocation—is a major consequence of the eleventh-century Gregorian Reform of the Church, under the influence of what Ghislain Lafont has called the "epistemology of illumination."[1] It is at this moment in history that hierarchy comes to be imagined as a "sacred order" of descending levels of power, in which knowledge and wisdom is passed down from higher to lower orders, and never in the opposite direction. Reflecting the neoplatonic vision of pseudo-Denis, the Church conceived of in this way is divided according to levels of power. Consequently, the laity—the lowest level—have no power at all, because there is no lower order to which to pass it along. In so many ways this understanding of hierarchy has remained with the Church until the very recent past and is reawakened in the increasingly strong efforts to reinterpret the message of Vatican II back into the mind-set of this earlier time or, as Cathleen Kaveny has described it in *Commonweal*, to read Vatican II through the sixteenth-century Council of Trent.[2]

Vatican II understood in some mysterious way that the time had come for the Church to recognize the historically conditioned character of the Gregorian Reform and bring itself into dialogue with a modern world in which hierarchy was not appreciated (*aggiornamento*) by going back behind that Gregorian Reform to the primacy of Spirit and charism that marked the Church of the first millennium (*ressourcement*). This is evident both in the pastoral tone of the sixteen documents that make up the paper record of the Council and in the major changes effected by the Council. Important among these are the reform of the liturgy, the revised understanding of revelation, the image of the Church as the people of God, the interpretation of the authority of the bishop in sacramental rather than in jurisdictional terms, and the new understanding of the role of the laity.

[1] Ghislain Lafont, *Imagining the Catholic Church: Structured Communion in the Spirit* (Collegeville, MN: Liturgical Press, 2000).

[2] Cathleen Kaveny, "Long Goodbye: Why Some Devout Catholics Are Leaving the Church," *Commonweal* (October 22, 2010).

One of the principal contributions of Vatican II was to return us to a richer understanding of baptism. Where baptism had come to be seen merely as a sacrament of initiation into the Church, the Council renewed attention to the idea of the baptismal *priesthood*. Before Vatican II and even today, if Catholics were surveyed to ascertain what they saw to be central to their tradition, we would be unlikely to find many choosing the priesthood of all the baptized. In part, this is because the baptismal priesthood is not preached and not even taught much. In part it is because the baptismal priesthood is the only priesthood that Luther recognized, and that fact was more than enough to consign it to the back burner of Catholic doctrine for several centuries. But its peculiar character is central to our coming to understand the one vocation but many roles of the Catholic Church.

In baptism we are all incorporated into a priestly people. The priesthood that is conferred on everyone in baptism is not directly connected to the ministerial or ordained priesthood that has been so central to ministry in the Catholic Church for very many centuries. The connection is not to ministerial priesthood, but to the priesthood of Jesus Christ, the "great High Priest" of the Letter to the Hebrews. Traditionally, the ordained priest represents Christ at the altar. But we are a priestly people, and that includes all the ordained, who have their ordained priesthood grafted onto a baptismal priesthood, which it does not replace. This priesthood is not about presiding at the Eucharist or leading the local community of faith, but rather about a life lived on the pattern of the life of Jesus, though it has a liturgical component. Just as Christ stands between God and the world, reconciling the two, so the priestly people who together are the sacrament of the presence of Christ in the world, stand in a reconciling role between God and the world.

Priesthood in the sense of baptismal priesthood is about action. To be a priestly people is to bring the cares of the world before God in the liturgy, and to carry the grace and strength received there back out into the world that is also a place of grace and salvation. So the image of baptism as donning a uniform with no further responsibilities is definitively abolished at Vatican II. Baptism is surely entry into a community, but it is into a community with a mission. We have the uniform in order to play the game. The uniform is the same for everyone, lay and ordained alike, and on the issue of mission there is no distinction between the starters and the bench players, between the first team and the reserves. Like kids soccer, *everybody* plays!

Each of us, from the lowliest believer to the pope himself, is baptized into mission. But what is the mission into which we have been baptized? What is the game that goes with the uniform we have acquired? In essence, it is to model our lives on Christ who came to serve, to sacrifice his life for the reconciliation of the world with God. Analogously, all Christians are called to the same responsibility, all Christians are "other Christs." Our sacrifice will most probably not involve a criminal's death on a cross, but it will be a making holy (the root meaning of "sacrifice") of our lives by giving them away. Other-centeredness is patterning our lives on Christ; self-centeredness is not.

If the center of mission lies in responsibility in the world, which all of us share in virtue of baptism, this has enormous consequences for our understanding of the respective roles of ordained and non-ordained Christians. To assert that the ordained are the only ones called to serve, or that they have a higher calling than the laity, is plain wrong. There is one calling to mission, entailed in baptism, but there may be many ways of living out this calling, and there is no justification for thinking of hierarchy as some kind of sliding scale of holiness or of the importance of the mission of one relative to another. The hierarchical vision of pseudo-Denis, in which only the higher can pass along grace, help, or power to the lower and the lower can do nothing for the higher, lies at the back of the conception of the role of clergy relative to laity that has dominated Catholic understandings of ministry for at least the last thousand years. The influence of this kind of thinking was detrimental if not catastrophic to a right understanding of the Church. Hierarchy has its root meaning not as "ordering" meaning ranking in importance but as "ordering to mission." We are all ordered to mission. We all have our place in this hierarchy. Since being ordered to mission is a consequence of baptism, we are all equally ordered to mission.

The understanding of mission has changed greatly in recent years because our understanding of the nature of the Church has been transformed, above all through the work of the Council fathers of Vatican II. Yves Congar wrote once that "final salvation will be achieved by a wonderful re-floating of our earthly vessel rather than by a transfer of the survivors to another ship wholly built by God."[3] In saying this he was breaking with many centuries of thinking in

[3] Congar, *Lay People in the Church*, 102.

which the role of the Church in mission, beyond itself, was in the nature of a fishing expedition or a safari. How many souls can we capture for Christ? How many pagans can we save by baptizing them? How many can we bring into the sheepfold where there is safety and light and salvation, freeing them from the darkness and ignorance of their ways as Jews, Muslims, Buddhists, and so on? These questions are now replaced by a simple, single query: how can we help the human world to come to a better knowledge of what human flourishing might be? St. Irenaeus famously wrote that "the glory of God is the human being fully alive."[4] How, then, can we aid human beings to be more fully alive, to live lives in which their full potential as human beings is explored? This is the challenge of mission in the modern world. The Church is best envisaged, from the perspective of mission, as a sacrament, or a sign of the love of God in and for the world that works by performing the love of God in and for the world. Thus shall we, with God's help, wonderfully refloat our earthly vessel. It is, after all, the world and not the Church alone that God wills to save.

So what are the particular responsibilities of the laity and the clergy relative to mission? Because we are all baptized and thus oriented to mission, and because there truly is only one mission, we are all called to mission, though not all in the same way. In the previous chapter we saw that the role of the laity, whose lives are lived out in the secular world and who are described by the Council fathers as "secular," is to be in the front line, the vanguard of the Church's divine mandate to work toward a progressively more human world, to bring human flourishing closer. The primary responsibility of the ordained is for the health of the community of faith, whose *raison d'être* is to give glory to God in worship and mission. Lafont puts this very well when he says that "the priest's mission is to stir up, verify, and coordinate these ministries in the Church and to gather them together in the unique sacrifice of Christ, whose mystery he proclaims personally in the homily."[5] Here is the wisdom of John Paul II's occasional worries about "the laicization of the clergy and the clericalization of the laity," though it is not clear that he was thinking so much about mission as about lifestyle and, perhaps,

---

[4] Irenaeus, *Against Heresies*, 4. 34. 5. See http://www.earlychurchtexts.com/public /irenaeus_glory_of_god_humanity_alive.htm.

[5] Lafont, *Imagining the Catholic Church*, 162.

about the peculiar situation of those whom we refer to as lay ecclesial ministers.[6] John Paul also went on record, before his election to the papacy, as believing that the central message of the Vatican Council was its statement that the two priesthoods differ "in essence and not only in degree." While it really is difficult to substantiate such a claim, it is important to establish that the two priesthoods are different, so that an ordained priest is not more a priest than the baptized lay person but has added another form of priesthood to the baptismal priesthood that can never be set aside.

If we are going to make this claim about mission and about the respective responsibilities of the ordained and those who are not ordained, then what does this suggest about the traditional understandings of clergy as somehow ontologically changed by their ordination to the diaconate and the priesthood? "Traditional," of course, is a term that often hides the fact that an idea or practice grew up for particular reasons in definite historical circumstances, and the so-called "character theology" of ordination is one of those cases. Lafont has written eloquently of how the Gregorian Reform of the Church (from the work of Gregory VII, pope from 1073 to 1085) saw the sacramental character of ordination as "a sacred instrumental power, immanent to the person of the priest and indelible," and of how over time the focus shifted from the permanence of the instrumental power to the being of the priest himself, so that he became "a Christian who existed on another ontological level than that defined by baptism and confirmation."[7] This is something we have now lived with for almost a thousand years, but this in itself does not mean that there is no other way to think of the role of ordination. What about the previous thousand years?

Lafont's book is eloquent about the importance of imagination in thinking about the future of the Church, but how true is it that the notion of the permanence of the instrumental power of the priest is any more essential to our understanding of priesthood than is the "substantial ontological change" traditionally supposed to occur at the moment of ordination? While it may be important that we think of some roles of the priest as inevitably if not essentially belonging to the office of the priest, once we remove the idea of substantial

---

[6] We will consider the situation of lay ecclesial ministers in the next chapter.

[7] Lafont, *Imagining the Catholic Church*, 59.

ontological change from our conception of ordination, it is hard to see why a priest must necessarily be permanently a priest. A good example to illustrate this is the situation of the resigned or former or "laicized" priest in the Church today. These "former" priests may have gone through a canonical process that involves their—telling phrase—"reduction to the lay state," but they remain priests in the eyes of the Church and in some circumstances are obliged to exercise their priestly role, for example, giving absolution to someone *in articulo mortis*. Aside from such extreme circumstances, however, their priesthood has been reduced to their ontological status devoid of any specific task and the permanence of their instrumental power is permanently suspended. It is not unreasonable to ask what this all means.

The "reduction to the lay state" of the former priest essentially makes him a hostage to the permanence of the priestly state, but at the same time it brings us back to reflection on the issue of vocation. As a member of the baptismal priesthood, the vocation to Christian discipleship is neither removed nor altered by laicization, though the arena in which it will be exercised changes from that of the Church internally to that of the Church at work in the secular world. If we insist on continuing to call ordination to priesthood an ontologically irreversible condition, then we introduce a distinction in kind between the vocation to the lay life and the vocation to priesthood, and we are back with the fundamental understanding that leaves us once again with a cultic vision of priesthood. If we abide with the conviction that there is one Christian vocation but many ways of living it out, then we leave room for understanding priesthood without the language of ontological change. But in the present dispensation we have priests who are permanently ontologically changed, other men with other callings who could, in principle, be admitted to the ranks of the ontologically changed, and women who, so they say, cannot. And, of course, there are those men—former priests—who have been ontologically changed and remain so but whose vocation is now to something other than that to which the ontologically changed are called. This is not a good picture.

A second test case for the value of notions of ontological change is afforded by reflecting on the vowed life in a religious order. Traditionally the Church has used the language of vocation to refer to religious in precisely the way it is used to refer to ordained ministers. Yet their situations are different. Religious qua religious are not ordained, though in fact many of the male religious are. Religious are vowed to celibacy while ordination requires only a promise "to obey the law of celibacy of the Western Church" and can be dispensed in some circumstances (the well-known example of married Episcopalian priests—only males, of course—who become Catholic and wish to continue to exercise their calling). Yet, it was the religious witness of celibacy that led eventually to the law of celibacy for the clergy. The way of life of the priest who is ontologically changed is in this respect at least patterned on the life of religious who are not ontologically changed. And here is the really difficult issue: surely the vocation to religious life is similarly dramatic to that of the priest and canonically, at least, it seems that with solemn vows there is a kind of permanence. Yet the vows can be dispensed, and the individual can return to lay life, and there is never any hint of substantial ontological change in the language surrounding religious profession.[8]

One of the more creative ways in which this whole question of ordained ministry has been addressed is by means of the concept of relationality. So in their different ways, to mention just two, both Richard Gaillardetz and Edward Hahnenberg have suggested that we replace the idea of substantial ontological change with that of relational ontological change.[9] While it is arguable that it is the word "ontological" that creates the bigger problem, the shift to "relational" is helpful. Essentially, the argument is that those who enter any form of ministry in the Church are placed in a new relationship to the rest of the community of faith. So the woman who was a mother of four one day becomes the CCD teacher for fifth-grade children, and those around her in the community now see the same person in a different light. The same relational change happens to the one who enters ordained ministry, though obviously the change is more dramatic because the one who was not presiding at ministry and

---

[8] Lafont has addressed this by proposing that religious consecration is sacramental and by suggesting, therefore, that the dispensation from solemn vows should be a much more attenuated process than it currently is. See *Imagining the Catholic Church*, 131–33.

[9] Richard R. Gaillardetz, "The Ecclesiological Foundations of Ministry within an Ordered Communion," in *Ordering the Baptismal Priesthood: Theologies of Lay and Ordained Ministry*, ed. Susan K. Wood (Collegeville, MN: Liturgical Press, 2003), 26–51. Edward P. Hahnenberg, *Ministries: A Relational Approach* (New York: Crossroad, 2003).

leading the community now is. In the Church at present, this ordination is permanent and doubtless that is the reason why the term
"relational ontological change" has been suggested as preferable to
"substantial ontological change." Either way, it is an irreversible
change in "being," but at least the focus is on relationality and not
on sacred power.

Thus far, we have seen that the fundamental vocation of all Christians is the one calling to follow Christ by participating in the Church
as the sacrament of the presence of the love of God in the world.
While there are many ways of fulfilling this one vocation, many
roles within the Church, it is difficult to make the case that one of
these ways involves irreversible ontological change while the others
do not. We have also examined two examples of situations that test
the coherence of the traditional approach to the clergy/laity distinction: the laicized priest and the vowed religious man or woman. So
how might we move beyond the impasse with which the present
situation leaves us?

While it does not seem helpful to distinguish the ways in which
different people live out the one Christian vocation, the need for
stability without absolute permanence, still more without ontological change, suggests revisiting the idea of different gifts or charisms.
Just as the character theology that developed in the Middle Ages
was an understandable development for its times, so it might be that
today we need to try something different, something which might
suit the times better. It is a commonplace to observe that our times
are allergic to permanence. People change occupations and locations
much more than they used to, and transience has also affected both
lifelong commitments to priestly ministry and, of course, to marriage.
While this possibly temporary cultural shift is no reason to adjust
Church teachings to fit the times, it might be more productive to
think about vocation less in the somewhat tarnished and abused category of permanence and more by reflecting on the notion of fidelity.

Charisms seem to fit better into the category of fidelity than that
of permanence. In Christian tradition they are drawn first from the
writings of St. Paul to the Corinthians, where he enumerates the
many gifts or talents that individuals are given by God for their own
personal development and for the good of the community. Evidently
our human and Christian fulfillment will be materially connected
to faithfulness to our God-given gifts. The more we exercise our
talents, the more we become the person we are, the one God wants

us to be. If we have the gift of prophecy, then we must prophesy for the good of the community of faith. The same is true if it is teaching or administration that is our personal strength. The test of the right use of these gifts is the foundational commandment to love. Even John Paul II, speaking of the importance of freedom of speech in the Church, makes this point about the prophetic voice. "Criticism is useful in the community," he said in a general audience he gave in June 1992, "which must always be reformed and must try to correct its own imperfections. In many cases it helps the community to take a new step forward. But if it comes from the Holy Spirit, criticism must be animated by the desire to advance in truth and love." This corresponds closely to the best way to formulate the relationship between charisms and love: the role we play in the Church must be the way each of us acts in fidelity to the one vocation to be the sacrament of the love of God in the world. We must act in fidelity to our charisms because this is also our fidelity to ourselves.

While fidelity to ourselves is the way we express our one Christian vocation, the self is no fixed thing. Here, the work of Lonergan is once again helpful. Because religion is about the relationship between God and the human person in the human community, says Lonergan, "any deepening or enriching of our apprehension of man possesses religious significance and relevance." Classically, he continues, the tradition understood the human person as a duality of body and soul, but today we add "the richer and more concrete apprehension of man as incarnate subject." The old understanding of the human person as a fixed body/soul duality must give way to the much more dynamic vision of the human person that modernity has acquired, above all through the human sciences. But if this is the case then we may also have to begin to think about what it means to be faithful to ourselves, if ourselves are understood in dynamic fashion, just as we have always had to pay attention to how to be faithful to a Church in which the dynamic element has always been present in the guise of tradition.[10]

Understanding the human self more dynamically as an incarnate subject is not problematic for our fundamental commitment to the one Christian calling, since of its nature it is open to our growing in it and into it as time passes and our wisdom and love grow. At any

---

[10] Bernard Lonergan, *A Second Collection*, 61.

given moment in life we commit ourselves in fidelity to the Gospel's demands on us to particular ways of being Christian and being human, but since the "I" that I am is dynamic, there can be no final certainty that this way of being faithful will not eventually give way to some other way. As we grow in wisdom or holiness or the capacity to love, new talents and gifts may emerge and others may wane as their usefulness to the self or the community of faith dissipates.

Some may feel that this is a picture of alarming fluidity in the ranks of ministers in the Church, as they slip from ministry to ministry, from charism to charism, as their needs for self-fulfillment—that lovely sixties word—are blamed on the Holy Spirit and a dysfunctional temporariness comes to infect the community of faith. The issue, of course, is one of discernment—that is, of discerning how the one vocation to faithfulness to the Gospel may need to be differently construed at different times in one's life. It is not self-fulfillment that is in question, but self-transcendence. Problems emerge, if the contemplated change of role is simultaneously a weakening of resolve in the self-transcendence of the one Christian vocation. But if marriage or ordination or religious life has become an exercise in the failure to transcend self, to a point where it is irremediable (and this point must never be too quickly assumed to have arrived), then change must be contemplated, however painful.

A further and final way to approach this question of the relationship between ordained and lay ministry is through looking a little more closely than we usually do at Vatican II's reworking of the relationship between the bishop and the priest and comparing it to the calling of lay people. As we saw in part 1 of this book, before the Council the priest was seen as the one with the fullness of orders, and the bishop was distinguished by his larger jurisdiction alone. Vatican II rethought the role of the bishop as the one with the "fullness of orders," which meant of course that they could not simply be related to the "power" to consecrate the bread and wine. Instead, it is clearly described as a matter of Christian spiritual leadership, of being Christ for the local church. The priest who does precisely the same thing in presiding at Eucharist shares in the bishop's sacramental ministry to be Christ to the community, but to a smaller section of the community. In other words, he presides at Eucharist, bishop or priest, because he is the spiritual leader of the local church. But lay mission and ministry is all about being Christ for the world, being the sacramental presence of Christ in the world that does not know him, being the leaven in the mass. Christ's headship, and Christ as present in one another, may in the end be more helpful ways to talk about the difference between the two priesthoods. Both represent Christ in their different ways.

In the end, then, the test of the rightness of the roles we play in the Church is their capacity to enable us in the one Christian vocation we all share. Because of our baptism and confirmation, we are all called to be the sacramental presence of the love of God in Christ for the world. The only question for each of us is just how we may best live that one vocation. Whether, in the abstract, one way is higher or better than the other is not worth thinking about and has caused a lot of harm in the history of the Church. For you or me, only one way is better, and that is what we have to find, or let it choose us, and live in fidelity to it. Which way is right for you or me is not something either of us can discern for the other. The only way is the way of self-transcendence for, as the Gospel has it, "Unless a grain of wheat falls into the earth and dies, it remains just a single grain" (John 12:24).

Chapter 6

Lay Ecclesial Ministers:
Are They Theological Monsters?

We cannot discuss the future of ministry in the Catholic Church without examining and analyzing the phenomenon of what has come to be called "lay ecclesial ministry," and yet we can neither easily classify lay ecclesial ministers nor locate them smoothly in traditional concepts of ministry. This is the reason that I have asked the question, is she or he a theological monster? A monster, of course, is not necessarily hideous, as anyone who saw Angelina Jolie's portrayal of Grendel's mother in the movie *Beowulf* can testify. Often the monster, by its very departure from the normal, will seem grotesque though it is perhaps the case that any genetic mutation, even one that will eventually survive and supplant that from which it emanated, will seem horrific. The new is often scary until it becomes the normal. *Homo sapiens* perhaps revolted the species that preceded it. Other monsters not so naturally produced, as in the laboratory of Dr. Frankenstein, arouse fear or loathing or even pity because they are artificial constructions, though again they may seem lovable to some. All these variations on what we take to be normal might suggest to us that monstrosity, like beauty, is in the eye of the beholder. Thus might they occasion caution in the face of the new. The lay ecclesial minister may, but may not, be a threat to either species—clergy or laity.

When we think about the emerging phenomenon of lay ecclesial ministers, our first tendency is to compare them with the clergy whose roles they have increasingly taken over, if not exactly usurped. They certainly perform many of the functions that were more or less exclusively the responsibility of ordained priests in the not-so-distant past. They read the lessons at Mass or distribute communion, they run prayer groups and direct adult faith formation, they have charge over parishes with no resident priest. Full-time or part-time, paid or volunteer, they exercise ministerial functions within the local community of faith. When we see them in this light, the question that comes to mind is how their ministry stands relative to that of the ordained priest, much of whose work they are now doing. Are they, indeed, mere stand-ins in what is in principle a temporary shortage of ordained clergy, or are they exercising a genuine ministerial calling? On the one side, the Church cannot comfortably imagine that a shortage of ordained ministers ought to be or will be a permanent feature, which would suggest that lay ecclesial ministers in the form in which we know them would in some way be temporary. On the other hand, if their work is indeed a genuine ecclesial calling, it is hard to imagine the Spirit calling them to the ministry of temporary stand-in. Are they, to employ the image we used earlier, bench players seeing, for whatever reason, rather more playing time than most would have expected? Or are they perhaps unknowing precursors of a radical restructuring of the rules of the game? If by some miracle the numbers of traditional priestly vocations shot up, would the lay ecclesial ministers return meekly to the bench and exercise their waiting ministry of availability once again? And would the Church expect that of them, even if—as is clearly the case—they exercise their ministry commendably? If, on the other hand, there is no return to large numbers of generous young men offering themselves for the celibate priesthood, at what point does the person from the bench become accepted as a genuine first-string player?

It is equally important, when contemplating the phenomenon of lay ecclesial ministers, to look at them relative to the laity as a whole. It is when we take this step that we see that the various roles lay ecclesial ministers exercise vis-à-vis the community, precisely because the rest of the laity do not take them up, are indeed genuinely vocational, callings by the Spirit to specific ministries. But if this true, then they are distinguished from the rest of the laity, just as they are distinct from traditional ordained ministers. Not (yet) clergy, not (any longer) laity, they live in some muddied middle realm, some twilight zone of priestly ambiguity, where their service to Christ's Church, for all that it is often much-appreciated, is frequently ill-understood. Lay ecclesial ministers are part of the American Catholic parochial landscape and it is increasingly true that the Church cannot function without them. To some they are the apostles of the second string, to others they are heralds of a new conception of priestly ministry. Which is the proper understanding of their role?

In a series of documents published over the past thirty years, the US Conference of Catholic Bishops has attempted to analyze and evaluate the growing phenomenon of the lay ecclesial minister. They began in 1980 with *Called and Gifted: The American Catholic Laity*, followed it fifteen years later with *Called and Gifted for the Third Millennium*, and in 2005 they added *Co-Workers in the Vineyard of the Lord: A Resource for Guiding the Development of Lay Ecclesial Ministry*.[1] In each case the discussion of the lay ecclesial minister is placed in the wider context of the baptismal call to mission that all lay people share. *Co-Workers* clearly states what it is that distinguishes the lay ecclesial minister proper: *authorization* of the hierarchy to serve publicly in the local church; *leadership* in a particular area of ministry; *close mutual collaboration* with the pastoral ministry of bishops, priests, and deacons; and *preparation and formation* appropriate to the level of responsibilities that are assigned to them. Lay ecclesial ministers are thus clearly distinguished from the general mission of the laity to the secular world—a role they exercise in virtue of their baptism and thus without the requirement of ecclesiastical oversight. Lay ecclesial ministers are evidently to be understood as ministerial insiders.

The treatment of lay ecclesial ministers in the three documents is notably varied. *Called and Gifted* welcomes them as "a gift to the Church" and "a new development," commenting that "all these lay ministers are undertaking roles that are not yet clearly spelled out."[2] In *Called and Gifted for the Third Millennium*, published in 1995, the bishops recognize the extraordinary growth in lay ministry, commenting that at least half of all parishes have vowed religious or lay people in "pastoral staff positions." They join pastors and parish-

---

[1] US Conference of Catholic Bishops, *Called and Gifted: The American Catholic Laity* (Washington, DC: USCCB Publishing, 1980), available at http://old.usccb.org/laity /called_and_gifted.pdf. USCCB, *Called and Gifted for the Third Millennium* (Washington, DC: USCCB Publishing, 1995), http://www.usccb.org/about/laity-marriage-family -life-and-youth/laity/called-and-gifted-for-the-third-millennium.cfm. USCCB, *Co-Workers in the Vineyard of the Lord* (Washington, DC: USCCB Publishing, 2006), http:// old.usccb.org/laity/laymin/co-workers.pdf.

[2] USCCB, *Called and Gifted*, 7.

ioners in "expressing gratitude for this development," noting that
lay ministers "speak of their work, their service, as a calling, not
merely a job."[3] The latest and lengthiest of the three documents,
Co-Workers in the Vineyard of the Lord (2005), is equally if not more
appreciative of the many forms of lay ministry, the bishops commenting that they "are very grateful for all who undertake various
roles in Church ministry."[4] Unlike the two previous documents, this
one has a lengthy theological discussion of the place of lay ministry
in the Church. The two poles of this discussion are, first, the close
connection between communion and mission, which incorporates
all the baptized into missionary activity and, second, the "primary
distinction" that "lies between the ministry of the lay faithful and
the ministry of the ordained, which is a special apostolic calling."[5]
The text continues in a manner that merits fuller quotation:

> Both are rooted in sacramental initiation, but the pastoral min-
> istry of the ordained is empowered in a unique and essential
> way by the Sacrament of Holy Orders. Through it, the ministry
> of the apostles is extended. As successors to the apostles, bishops
> "with priests and deacons as helpers" shepherd their dioceses as
> "teachers of doctrine, priests for sacred worship and ministers of
> government." The work of teaching, sanctifying, and governing
> the faithful constitutes the essence of apostolic ministry; it forms
> "an indivisible unity and cannot be understood if separated one
> from the other." This recognition of the unique role of the or-
> dained is not a distinction based on merit or rank; rather, it is
> a distinction based on the sacramental character given by the
> Holy Spirit that configures the recipient to Christ the Head and
> on the particular relationship of service that Holy Orders brings
> about between ecclesiastical ministry and the community. The
> ordained ministry is uniquely constitutive of the Church in a
> given place. All other ministries function in relation to it.[6]

The theological discussion of lay ministry in the second and third of
these documents is reflective of John Paul II's anxieties over the twin
dangers of "the clericalization of the laity and the laicization of the
clergy," signaled in his apparent belief that the key to Vatican II was

---

[3] USCCB, *Called and Gifted for the Third Millennium*, 17.
[4] USCCB, *Co-Workers*, 10.
[5] Ibid., 21.
[6] Ibid., 21–22.

its insistence that the ordained and baptismal priesthood differ in essence and not merely in degree, though they are intimately related to
one another, and worked out most fully in the postsynodal apostolic
exhortation *Christifideles Laici.*[7] These concerns are also most evident
in John Paul II's 1999 apostolic exhortation *Ecclesia in America.* While
lay ecclesial ministers are not referred to directly as such, the pope
recognizes "a second area in which many lay faithful are called to
work" beyond the sanctification of the secular world, "and this can
be called 'intra-ecclesial.'" The subject is dealt with very delicately,
especially the synod fathers' hope "that the Church would recognize
some of these works as lay ministries, with a basis in the Sacraments
of Baptism and Confirmation, without compromising the specific
ministries proper to the Sacrament of Orders." While not rejecting
this request outright, John Paul II is insistent on the need to avoid
"any confusion with the ordained ministries and the activities proper
to the Sacrament of Orders, so that the common priesthood of the
faithful remains clearly distinguished from that of the ordained." The
works entrusted to lay people must be "clearly 'distinct from those
which constitute steps on the way to the ordained ministry' [quoting
the synod's recommendations to the pope] and which are carried
out by candidates for the priesthood before ordination," and care
must be taken to ensure that it goes hand in hand with the activity
proper to the laity, in which their place cannot be taken by priests:
the area of temporal realities."[8]

A theology of lay ecclesial ministry will have to deal with several
profound theological issues that are either not raised by the Vatican
or the USCCB, or raised and dismissed in perfunctory fashion. In
the first instance, the bishops seem reluctant to use the language of
"vocation" to describe the calling of the lay ecclesial minister. In *Co-
Workers*[9] they use the term vocation for the universal call to discipleship and for the lay vocation in general, but they sidestep the issue
of a specific calling to lay ecclesial ministry, suggesting that further

[7] John Paul II, *The Vocation and Mission of the Lay Faithful in the Church and in the World* (December 30, 1988), http://www.vatican.va/holy_father/john_paul_ii/apost_exhortations/documents/hf_jp-ii_exh_30121988_christifideles-laici_en.html.

[8] John Paul II, *Ecclesia in America* (January 22, 1999), 44, http://www.vatican.va/holy_father/john_paul_ii/apost_exhortations/documents/hf_jp-ii_exh_22011999_ecclesia-in-america_en.html.

[9] Quoting *Christifideles Laici* 23.

thought needs to be given to this issue. Their position is clearly stated, though somewhat mystifying: "Lay ecclesial ministry is exercised in accordance with the specific lay vocation." But what does this mean if the ministry itself is in all respects similar to priestly ministry and not at all an exercise of that "secular" character of the apostolate in the world? While it is clear that the bishops are unwilling or unable to move away from the language of "qualitative difference" to describe ordained ministry, withholding the term "vocation" from genuinely ministerial work, to which, presumably, the Spirit calls the individual, does not seem to be the way to accomplish it. The preference for the word "call" over the word "vocation" is quite unhelpful, since the two words are synonymous. If the bishops wish to insist consistently on some essential difference between ordained and lay ministry, then they would be wise to find something more secure than a dubious distinction between two words that mean the same to justify what is apparently so important to them. If they wish to avoid the implication that the distinction is simply functional—as they do—then they must find a way to assert that ordained ministry is a different *kind* of call or a call *of a higher order* to make their position more secure. In fact, all they offer in this regard is reference to the sacramental basis of ordained ministry and the claim that "all other ministries function in relation to it," which seems little more than the bald assertion of what precisely is placed in question by the emergence of the lay ecclesial ministers.

Second, the bishops explicitly deny that lay ecclesial ministry is a new rank or order in the Church: "Lay ecclesial minister is not itself a specific position title. We do not use the term in order to establish a new rank or order among the laity." It is a term they intend purely descriptively to cover those many ministries conducted within the Church by officially appointed lay people. Since lay ecclesial ministers on the American model are not a universal phenomenon and even where they exist they are often described differently or not at all, the bishops seem to be on solid ground here. On the other hand, if we imagine them as an emerging phenomenon whose theological significance will only become apparent over time, it could be premature to declare them not this or not that. Indeed, if we adopt the more sophisticated understanding of hierarchy as denoting order rather than rank, then the new position a lay minister acquires in virtue of being commissioned for or appointed to some particular ministry may have implications for hierarchical ordering. If, of course, hierarchy is taken to mean simply rank, then lay ecclesial ministers *would* be the creation of a new form or hybrid somehow between lay people and clergy.

The third question relates to the significance of the same work conducted by two people, one ordained and one not. Writing of the work of deacons, another ecclesial group whose theological warrants are less than clear, the bishops say, "While at times deacons may carry out some of the same tasks as lay ecclesial ministers, care must be taken to avoid a merely functional understanding of the deacon's sacramental identity."[10] Distinguishing the deacon from the lay minister or priest, the claim is made that "even when functions may be exercised that are the same as those exercised by lay persons or by priests, the deacon's ministry nonetheless has a distinct sacramental basis that flows from the Sacrament of Orders."[11] It is difficult to see what exactly is added on to the same function by the "distinct sacramental basis." If I exercise a ministry as an ordained deacon or as a commissioned lay minister, what's the difference? Or is it that the old character-theology is lurking here in the assertion, perhaps, that the difference is that the deacon has, through ordination, become a new kind of person?

If the USCCB has not yet grappled with the theological complexity of the issues surrounding lay ecclesial ministry, there are several other directions in which to look for aid. They include Congar's life-long, developing understanding of a theology of the laity, Rahner's reflections on when a minister is a lay person and when not,[12] and Leonardo Boff's discussion of lay leadership in his book *Ecclesiogenesis: The Base Communities Re-invent the Church*.[13] Taken together, they suggest directions for further thinking.

Congar's *Lay People in the Church*[14] was written decades before lay ecclesial ministry came into existence. Nevertheless he reflected at length in this major work among others on the significance of "the cooperation of the laity in the hierarchical apostolate," to borrow

---

[10] USCCB, *Co-Workers*, 22.

[11] Ibid.

[12] See especially Rahner, "Notes on the Lay Apostolate" in *Theological Investigations II: Man in the Church* (Baltimore: Helicon, 1963), 319–52.

[13] Leonardo Boff, *Ecclesiogenesis: The Base Communities Re-invent the Church* (Maryknoll, NY: Orbis, 1986).

[14] Congar, *Lay People in the Church*.

the phrase Pius XII used to describe Catholic Action. Congar saw three forms of apostolic activity. One, in virtue of baptism alone and conducted without ecclesiastical approval or oversight, was located in the individual lay Catholic's life in the world, in which the individual taught and shared God's love simply through the force of holy living. At the other extreme was ordained ministry. But between the two was Catholic Action, coordinated apostolic activity of groups of lay people done in the name of the Church, and hence licensed and supervised by the hierarchical ministers themselves. Writing in Europe in the 1950s, Congar probably made more of this phenomenon than history has shown it to deserve, but it is certainly true that it was in Catholic Action that large numbers of lay people first began to exercise significant leadership in pastoral ministry. Today, while lay ecclesial ministers are not organized in associations with specific pastoral objectives, as Catholic Action had been, they are often seen in a precisely similar fashion "cooperating" in the hierarchical apostolate.

Congar's later writings suggest thinking again about the connotations of lay ministry as "cooperation" in the hierarchical apostolate. In the first instance we should take note of his reflections on the ministry as a whole. In three important essays written in the 1960s, Congar moves decisively away from the clergy/laity dualism that had marked *Lay People in the Church* and that he had begun to correct in the revised edition of that work published during the Council.[15] Summing up his own shift of thought, Congar wrote in 1972 that "Jesus has instituted a structured community which is as an entirely holy, priestly, prophetic, missionary, apostolic; it has ministries at the heart of its life, some freely raised up by the Spirit, others linked by the imposition of hands to the institution and mission of the Twelve."[16] And he famously added, as we saw earlier, that after the Council "it is no longer the layman who stands in need of definition, but the priest."[17]

Congar's most helpful insight, however, is on apostolicity. We tend to think of apostolicity as a characteristic of bishops, or at least of the

---

[15] Congar, "*Ministères et laïcat dans les recherches actuelles de la théologie catholique romaine,*" *Verbum Caro* 18 (1964): 127–48; "Ministères et structuration de l'Eglise3," *La Maison Dieu* 102 (1970): 7–20; "Quelques problèmes touchant les ministers," *Nouvelle revue théologique* 93 (1971): 785–800.

[16] Congar, "My Pathfindings in the Theology of Laity and Ministries," *The Jurist* 2 (1972): 178. This passage, incidentally, is quoted by Leonardo Boff in *Ecclesiogenesis*, p. 29.

[17] Congar, "My Pathfindings," 181–82.

ordained, when in fact it is a mark of the entire Church. Referring to circumstances in Nazi-occupied Europe, in which the laity perforce often took upon themselves apostolic work more commonly associated with ordained ministers, Congar observes that the reason for this is not simply a shortage of clergy. On the contrary, "it is because there is a qualitative insufficiency in the pastoral field, an intrinsic ineffectiveness in the apostolic set-up, if the laity is not organically associated in the work of the gospel—not just a few of the laity, 'safe people,' but the Christian laity taken as a whole." The nature of the modern world, Congar comments wisely, is that, more and more, pastoral necessity will make us see that "the work of the gospel be considered as belonging not to the clergy alone but to the clergy and the laity together."[18] By reading the signs of the times in this way, Congar is referred back to ancient understandings of the nature of apostolicity, lost to the Church for centuries. He writes approvingly of John Chrysostom's idea that "the laity form the priestly *pleroma* of the bishop."

While Congar did not live to see the development of lay ecclesial ministers in any formal sense, there can be little doubt that he would have welcomed it. The crucial point he is making about apostolicity is not that our times are short of priests and so laity can and must take up the slack, but that because our times are short of priests, it becomes progressively clearer that apostolic activity in its fullness requires the involvement of the laity. The relative profusion of priests in the past has served to hide the apostolicity of the laity. Today we can see that there is a lot of room for truly apostolic work by the nonordained *within* the Church, just as Congar saw the same need being met in directly pastoral activity *outside* the Church. Apostolicity is a characteristic of the whole community of faith, possessed by the laity in virtue of baptism, not delegated by the clergy because of some short or even long-term need. And if so, then we may need to turn back to the words of *Co-Workers*, which link the special character of priestly ministry to its apostolic origins, and ask if this is adequate.

But are the nonordained who are working in ministry inside the Church truly lay people? This is the question that Karl Rahner reflected on at length. In Rahner's view, "the lay state in the proper sense ceases whenever there is real and habitual participation in the

---

[18] Congar, *Lay People in the Church*, 374.

powers of the hierarchy in such a way that the exercise of these powers characterizes the life of such a person, i.e., determines his station in life," and that "it is theologically indifferent" whether these powers come from ordination "or are . . . bestowed without it."[19] This kind of hierarchical commission, which cannot be imposed on the individual, is an "apostolic sending-out," an act which "suppresses the apostle's original status in the world . . . and founds a new state and calling, with a new place in the world for the apostle and his own life, allocated to him by his very mission." Rahner's examples of such a person are instructive: "An officially-commissioned 'lay catechist,' a woman officially employed as 'parochial helper,' an official sacristan, etc. are not indeed ordained; yet if these are their principal functions, they are no longer, properly speaking, lay persons."[20] Indeed, for Rahner, the Church's act of commissioning such people, and their responsibilities very clearly represent what today we would call lay ecclesial ministers, makes them clerics, though it does not make them members of the hierarchy. In fact, Rahner seems to see them as equivalent to the ranks of married deacons (writing before Vatican II reintroduced this possibility in the Church), or even as a kind of diaconal ministry itself. He writes: "There are many tasks in the realm of the Church's apostolate as a whole which cannot be fulfilled on the plane of the lay apostolate; it would be necessary rather to create a new theological, psychological and legal sphere for them, on the level of the hierarchical apostolate."[21]

A more radical consideration of the issue of lay ministry is afforded in Boff's *Ecclesiogenesis*. Boff has very little to say about the lay apostolate in general and makes no reference to lay ecclesial ministry; however, he helps us think about the close relationship there is between our governing image of Church and the theological implications of lay ecclesial ministry. Boff's analysis, of course, is predicated upon the base community structure so alive in Brazil at the time of his writing. While initially the extent of lay leadership in the base communities was simply a practical pastoral necessity brought on by the lack of access to ordained ministers that huge segments of the Brazilian poor experienced, in Boff's book the ground has shifted to an emerging vision of a Church permanently structured around

---

[19] Rahner, "Notes on the Lay Apostolate, 330.
[20] Ibid., 335.
[21] Ibid., 337.

the base Christian community in which hierarchy takes its place as an important function within "the church as faith community," a Church that "was born not only from the opened side of Christ, but from the Holy Spirit, as well, on the day of Pentecost."[22] In this respect, Boff is entirely consistent with Congar's views on apostolicity quoted earlier. A shortage of priests clarifies the importance of lay apostolicity—it does not simply require it as a temporary expedient. And to the degree that this is true, it speaks directly to the situation of the American Church at the present day, where the declining numbers of ordained priests in active ministry has more or less been surpassed by the increasing numbers of lay ecclesial ministers. Moreover, just as in the Latin American situation, the leaders in lay ecclesial ministry are overwhelmingly women. Taken overall, Boff's view encourages us to look at the growth of lay ministry within the Church against the larger background of ministry as a whole, not simply in the dualistic categories that a hierarchical conception of Church encourages, if not necessitates.

The question with which all of these observations leave us is obvious enough: is the phenomenon of lay ecclesial ministry simply an example of what has been called "the apostolate of the second string" (the "reserves"), whose well-meaning and generous efforts will fill a hopefully temporary gap until the "real" players, the *starters*, the *first team*, can take up their rightful roles again? Or is this the work of the Holy Spirit, bringing about the new life that is so sorely needed in a Church whose current situation, to borrow words of Bryan Massingale, looks very much like hospice care? The US bishops have been commended for their most recent document on lay ministry, *Co-Workers in the Vineyard of the Lord*, and there is surely much of value in it. In particular, the focus on the symbiotic union of communion and mission is something to celebrate. However, once the document turns to discussing the relations between ordained and lay ecclesial ministry, there is little other than the reassertion of the essential distinction between the ordained and baptismal priesthood, which, however true it may be in the abstract, is profoundly unhelpful for figuring out the precise meaning of lay ecclesial ministry. While keeping the lay ecclesial minister firmly on the lay side of the clergy/laity divide, the document asserts a kind of "lay person–plus," men-

---

[22] Boff, *Ecclesiogenesis*, 24.

tioning the "special grace" that is apparent in the "call" (though not the "vocation") of those lay people who become ecclesial ministers.

The three authorities we have discussed above would address this issue differently. Congar calls on us to abandon the clergy/laity talk and substitute a kind of ministerial spectrum along which everyone, presumably, can find a place. Rahner bluntly asserts that the lay ecclesial minister is not a lay person but a cleric, though not a priest. And Boff evidently believes that the "lay coordinator" might be an extraordinary minister of the Eucharist, adding the question: "But what if, as in Latin America, the extraordinary becomes ordinary, normal, regular?"[23] What indeed? And what if the extraordinary should become the ordinary in New Ulm or even in New York?

So what kind of a monster is the lay ecclesial minister? At the present time, it would seem, she or he is the creation of Frankenstein, an amalgam of clerical and lay roles that are stitched together in a most unsatisfactory way. Maybe, given time and patience and work that is not motivated simply by shoring up outmoded distinctions, the Church may come to see this individual more as a promising genetic mutation, one that may carry the evolution of the Church a step further. We cannot conclude without pointing out that the etymological derivation of the word "monster" leads us back to the Latin in which the word could mean a portent or an omen. The lay ecclesial minister is surely a portent of the Church that is struggling to be reborn.

[23] Ibid., 70.

PART 3

In Search of a Humbler Church

□ □ □

We think today of Jesus, who always wants us all to be closer to Him, we think of the Holy People of God, a simple people, who want to get closer to Jesus, and we think of so many Christians of goodwill who are wrong and that instead of opening a door they close the door of goodwill. . . . So we ask the Lord that all those who come to the Church find the doors open, find the doors open, open to meet this love of Jesus.

—Pope Francis's homily, Casa Santa Marta,
May 25, 2013

Chapter 7

Salvation and the Religious Other

Preliminary Remarks on Ecclesial Humility

When people ask me what I do for a living and want to know more than the fact that I teach, I often say that I am that most unfortunate of human beings—a Roman Catholic ecclesiologist. This whimsical remark should be balanced against what I tell my students who ask me why they should study the Church. It may not always be pleasant, I reply, but it's never dull. And truly, the life of an ecclesiologist today is usually lively, maybe too lively, though measured only against other academic careers, of course. What is lively to a theologian might be deadly dull to a plumber or a neurologist. However, one truly never knows quite what tomorrow will bring. One of the reasons this branch of theology could be considered hazardous is that we ecclesiologists employ a largely contextual and inductive approach that runs substantially counter to the institutional face of Roman Catholicism. The papal magisterium continues to be wedded to a deductive method reflecting its ongoing commitment to the priority of the global over the local Church. But if there is something of an impasse between ecclesiology and officialdom, it is not going to be overcome in a knock-down, drag-out, head-to-head confrontation on some or all of the hot-button issues in Church life. Instead, what we need today is a large dose of humility, both toward one another in the increasingly polarized community of faith and also in our relations with the wider world beyond the Church. The two are connected, but here we will primarily focus on the need for ecclesial humility in face of the world beyond the Church.

Why should we focus on the virtue of humility? One important reason is that many of our ecclesial ills today are products of the sin of exclusion and can be addressed by attention to the virtue of humility. Whether we are engaged in invidious and often ignorant comparisons between the holy Church and the sinful world, or spiritually empty comparisons between the fullness of truth in "our" tradition and the defects of others, we are about the business of exclusion, sweeping aside God's holy mystery to impose our fallible human considerations about where "the true Church" can be found. It is a heresy, if not an actual crime, when a subgroup of the community of faith, in the name of its convictions of what purity looks like and persuaded that it can speak for God, marginalizes others, whether they are the divorced or gays and lesbians or religious sisters going about their jobs or whether they are working in Catholic hospitals or in Congress or, indeed, even if they are just theologians. It is, in fact, the old and dangerous heresy of Donatism.

In pursuit of a church that does not practice exclusion, this final part of the book will explore several facets of the ecclesial virtue of humility. We will move forward in three steps. After these few preliminary remarks we need to look at what *Lumen Gentium* has to say that is relevant to the discussion of ecclesial humility. We will find it in the discussion of the relationship of salvation in Christ to the truth of other religious traditions addressed in sections 13–17, and in the important image of "the pilgrim church." Second, we will turn to some examples of the relationship between humility and openness to the other, beginning with one drawn from the writings of Flannery O'Connor, of how God teaches the lesson of true humility to a person who exemplifies the sin of self-righteousness and the practice of exclusion and continuing with a brief series of meditations on the parable of the Good Samaritan, aided in this by some distinctions offered in the writings of Archbishop Rowan Williams. In the final chapter of the book we will try to draw all our reflections on *Lumen Gentium* into a proposal for an ecclesiology of humility. Our objective is a vision of a Church that is a whole lot less sure of itself than, at least on the surface, our Roman Catholic Church purports to be.

Attention to the need for ecclesial humility is not new, but it has quite recently been given renewed consideration in Gerard Mannion's book *Ecclesiology and Postmodernity: Questions for the Church in Our Time*[1] and in a collection of essays on the problem of exclusion

---

[1] Gerard Mannion, *Ecclesiology and Postmodernity: Questions for the Church in Our Time* (Collegeville, MN: Liturgical Press, 2007).

in Church practice.[2] "The postmodern *aggiornamento* of ecclesiology, of mission and practice," writes Mannion, "cannot be effectively achieved without ecclesial humility."[3] Mannion's point, indeed, is crucial; any *aggiornamento* encounters a world open, at its best, to dialogue and completely uninterested in dogmatic proclamation. In Rowan Williams's felicitous distinction mentioned earlier, the contemporary world with which Christians can enter into dialogue will be one that evinces procedural and not programmatic secularism—that is, its method is one in which "religious convictions are granted a public hearing in debate," though not necessarily any privilege.[4] By the same token, the Church in dialogue with this secular world must itself discover a kind of procedural rather than programmatic manner of proceeding. If ecclesial humility is possible, it will accept these conditions and require that others do the same. As I put it in a previous work:

> Is it possible to understand the fundamentals of Christian theology as lying *behind* the human person and the community, so to speak, forming the rhetorical background out of which the tradition encounters the world, rather than placed *in front of* the person and the community, as a blueprint for history or a program for the reform of the world?[5]

The need for humility in dialogue between church and world is indisputable, at least in the obvious sense that without it true dialogue is quite impossible. All genuine dialogue entails a willingness to change if it is not simply perlocutionary in Jürgen Habermas's sense, a strategic subterfuge often aimed at achieving ends other than those that would be arrived at by a commitment to open discourse.[6]

---

[2] Dennis M. Doyle, Timothy J. Furry, and Pascal D. Bazzell, eds., *Ecclesiology and Exclusion: Boundaries of Being and Belonging in Postmodern Times* (Maryknoll, NY: Orbis, 2012).

[3] Mannion, *Ecclesiology and Postmodernity*, 134.

[4] Rowan Williams, "Secularism, Faith and Freedom" (address to the Pontifical Academy of Social Sciences, 2006).

[5] Paul Lakeland, *Postmodernity: Christian Identity in a Fragmented World* (Minneapolis: Fortress, 1997), 91.

[6] Habermas adopted this term from J. L. Austin, see *How To Do Things with Words* (Cambridge: Cambridge University Press, 1962), and employed it extensively in his speech-act theory developed in the two volumes of *The Theory of Communicative Action: Reason and the Rationalization of Society*, vol. 1 (Boston: Beacon, 1984), and *The Theory of Communicative Action: Lifeworld and System*, vol. 2 (Boston: Beacon, 1988).

Three further questions arise. Can any institution committed to the defense of a metanarrative allow itself to employ anything more than the appearance of humility, if true humility means a readiness to admit that we are open to correction? Is humility still a virtue to be desired in the proclamation of magisterial teaching and, if so, what would it look like? Is humility vis-à-vis the world and vis-à-vis the community of faith theologically warranted and, if so, how? A few thoughts on each will conclude these preliminary reflections.

There are so many examples available of the missteps occasioned by the failure to tap into what Margaret Farley has so aptly called "the grace of self-doubt."[7] The principal example Mannion discusses is the 2000 Declaration of the Congregation for the Doctrine of the Faith, "On the Unicity and Salvific Universality of Jesus Christ and the Church," usually referred to simply as *Dominus Iesus*.[8] Whether or not it is true that this document was primarily addressed to Catholic theologians toying with the question of the universal salvific significance of Jesus Christ, the ecumenical fallout was considerable, tempered only by the good sense of our non-Catholic brothers and sisters who have heard this kind of thing so many times before, even if perhaps in the light of Vatican II they thought they had heard it for the last time. The document affirms that non-Catholic Christian communities "suffer from defects" (17). Non-Christian religions receive similar treatment: "If it is true that the followers of other religions can receive divine grace, it is also certain that objectively speaking they are in a gravely deficient situation in comparison with those who, in the Church, have the fullness of the means of salvation" (22). Buddhists and Baptists alike were afforded a glimpse into the way that Rome understood the limits of dialogue and could be forgiven for wondering what, in the end, the Catholic Church has to dialogue about. Surely, totalizing claims can leave little room for movement. How can the one true Church meet defective "ecclesial communities" on a level playing field, and how, indeed, can monotheism be anything other than intolerant of the truth claims of other religions?

---

[7] Margaret A. Farley, "Ethics, Ecclesiology and the Grace of Self-Doubt," in *A Call to Fidelity: On the Moral Theology of Charles E. Curran*, ed. James J. Walter, Timothy E. O'Connell, and Thomas A. Shannon (Washington, DC: Georgetown, 2002), 55–76.

[8] Congregation for the Doctrine of the Faith, *Dominus Iesus*, http://www.ewtn.com/library/curia/cdfunici.htm.

The answer, of course, is "only humbly." Humility in dialogue is not achieved with an assumption of the moral or spiritual superiority of the dialogue partner any more than it is in the assumption of our own fast-track to the truth. It is, rather, a matter of recognizing the holy mystery within which we all stand and which relativizes every perspective. It was this attitude, I think, which led Rahner beyond the encouraging wording of *Lumen Gentium* that saw all human beings as "somehow incorporated in or related to" the people of God, to his stated opinion that these words imply "the possibility of a properly salvific revelation-faith even beyond the Christian revelatory word."[9] So does the answer to my first question about how to be humble when protecting a metanarrative lie perhaps in undermining the "meta" by relating to a mystery that goes beyond all narratives?

Fast-forwarding to today and narrowing our gaze to the US Church over the last couple of years, we can see many examples of the damage that comes from failing to recognize the limitations to which even episcopal teaching is subject. In part 1 of this book we looked at a number of examples of the US bishops coming close to overreaching themselves in exercising their legitimate voice in public policy matters. We could also examine the apparent abandon with which certain individual bishops choose to fling around the threat of excommunication, and to act on it at times. And we could see all this alongside the continuing unwillingness to confront the true extent of episcopal culpability in the ongoing disclosures of sexual abuse.

When we start to look around for an explanation of the flaccidity of Church leadership in our times, we are drawn back to Mannion's identification of the vital importance of dialogue for a future ecclesiology, though this does not entirely answer the question of what, then, is to be done. Perhaps in Church leadership as in other walks of life, the more you know the more complex becomes the answer; the most dangerous kind of church leader is the one who does not know what he does not know and consequently doesn't know when to speak and when to be silent. As I said earlier in this book, I am also sure that teachers in the Church, just as teachers anywhere else, should recognize that if teaching is not effective the probability is that it is not due to the obtuseness of the student but

---

[9] "Towards a Fundamental Theological Interpretation of Vatican II," in *Vatican II: The Unfinished Agenda*, ed. Lucien Richard with Daniel Harrington and John W. O'Malley (New York/Mahwah, NJ: Paulist, 1987), 9–21. This quotation is from p. 14.

rather to the opacity of the pedagogy. If your students just don't get it, not the odd one but many or even most of them, then consider the possibility that you are teaching the wrong thing or perhaps the right thing in an ineffective way. Don't just repeat yourself or, still worse, raise your voice. Respect for your audience requires humility.

There is, however, a more disquieting concern that was hinted at in an editorial in *Horizons* when editor Anthony Godzieba wrote that he detected "a whiff of Donatism" in the attitudes of some US bishops to their responsibilities as teachers and leaders. Donatism in the looser sense, of course, is the demand for purity that can so easily become confidence in the purity of oneself and one's own kind, and which is certainly "in the air" whenever—as in the present moment—not a few bishops seem to look with equanimity on the possibility of a smaller and more obedient American Catholic Church, shorn of its impure dissenters. This kind of impulse, the misplaced "enthusiasm" that Ronald Knox saw to be the root of all heresy, begins in a worthy impulse toward spiritual perfection and ends—if there is no humility—in the "us versus them" of schism.[10] In Donatism it was bishops themselves who went into schism.

In the end, these journalistic observations have to give way to theological convictions, and Knox is again helpful in this regard. Reflecting on the implicit separatism of enthusiasm, Knox saw its roots in a different theology of grace. While our tradition sees grace perfecting nature, for the enthusiast "grace has destroyed nature, and replaced it." In particular, "he decries the use of human reason as a guide to any sort of religious truth" and accepts secular authority only on sufferance: "Always the enthusiast hankers after a theocracy, in which the anomalies of the present situation will be done away, and the righteous bear rule openly."[11] We should reflect on whether our present situation may not come close to this condition. Knox's picture, by the way, is very similar to Rahner's depiction of "the heresy of integrism," where Church teaching is understood as a kind of "template for secular society."[12]

[10] R. A. Knox, *Enthusiasm: A Chapter in the History of Religion* (Oxford: Oxford University Press, 1950), 3.

[11] Ibid.

[12] "Church and World," in *Sacramentum Mundi: An Encyclopedia of Theology*, vol. 1 of 6, ed. Karl Rahner (New York: Herder and Herder, 1969–70), 346–56.

The fundamental theological issue in fostering the grace of self-doubt, even among the official teachers in the Church, is the recognition that the grace of God is spread throughout the world, that it is not coextensive with the Church, and, indeed, that there is worldly grace that the Church does not control or even know. When grace is seen as the work of the Spirit and not as the preserve of the Church, there is absolutely no option but that of humility, both before the world and in face of the worldly experience of the Catholic laity whose vocation, Vatican II assured us, is "essentially secular." This perception that the grace of God is at work in the world is clear in the teaching of the Council on the universal call to salvation, to which we now turn.

What Does *Lumen Gentium* Say about Universal Salvation?

One of my favorite moments teaching undergraduates about the Second Vatican Council occurs when we come to consider the question raised in *Lumen Gentium* of who, exactly, is saved. Young Catholic men whose late adolescent rites of passage seem to require highly infrequent attendance at Mass or less than rigid conformity to the sexual ethical teaching of the Church look distinctly uneasy when I read to them the line that singles out seriously unfaithful Catholics as "those [who] could not be saved" (14). I let them dangle for a while before introducing the notion of formal contempt, and the sigh of relief is palpable. After all, if we feel guilty then we haven't cut all ties, and the severe words of the bishops probably don't apply to us. In any case, the final test of Church membership, we are rapidly learning, can be neither frequent church attendance nor close conformity to every jot and tittle of current Catholic teaching on sexual ethics—at least not unless we are ready for the Church to say farewell to most of its youth and many of its adult members.

The way the Council fathers treat the issue of the relationship between salvation in Christ and the message of other great world religions is one of the many points where Vatican II simply departed from longstanding convictions. Having proclaimed that the mission of the people of God is to work for the inclusion of all humanity within it, for the people of God "prefigures and promotes universal peace," section 13 ends with the extraordinary statement that "to it belong, or are related in different ways: the catholic faithful, others who believe in Christ, and finally all humankind, called by God's grace to salvation." While this is an important watershed and makes quite clear that the Church cannot look out on the rest of the world in terms of "us" and "them," the recognition of the universal call to salvation is not only theologically rich but also potentially perilous. How can the Church proclaim the relationship of all people to the one Church of Christ that "this pilgrim church is required for salvation" without relativizing the wisdom and truth of other faiths? How can it say that "Christ alone is mediator and the way of salvation" (14), without sounding complacent or triumphalistic? This is the challenge of sections 14–17.

It will be good, then, to begin our consideration with the distinctly unpromising declaration at the beginning of section 14 that "this pilgrim church is required for salvation." We shall have more to say about the image of pilgrim a little later; for now let us concentrate on the necessity of the Church. Some of the severity of this statement is ameliorated by pointing out that it is made in the context of considering Catholics themselves, so that the paragraph ends with a very sober note that comes as close as Vatican II ever came to the condemnatory anathemas of previous Councils:

> Those could not be saved who refuse either to enter the church, or to remain in it, while knowing that it was founded by God through Christ as required for salvation. (14)

The point of this statement is not that lukewarm Catholics are in danger of losing their eternal salvation, nor even that someone who follows his or her conscience into the Unitarian Church or becomes a Buddhist is being condemned. This is a statement that applies to Don Giovanni or Faust and to anyone else who in the full possession of faith decides to reject it. Knowing it to be true, he or she abandons it for some earthly reward or simply because of a clear calculus that a life of self-centeredness here and now is to be preferred to one in which the Gospel call to otherness must be recognized. The bishops are reiterating here the ancient condemnation of "formal contempt" for the truth of the Gospel. To fall into this trap you must be a believer marked by cold cynicism to an infinite degree.

Once this is cleared up we are still left with the very different statement that the Church is required for salvation, a statement made in the context of discussing the faith of Catholics but clearly intending a more universal application. However, it is particularly important to note that the bishops are not saying that membership of the Church is necessary for salvation. Their point is more cosmic; the Church, they effectively say, is a reality without which God's will for the salvation of the world would not be fulfilled. This is not as hubristic as it might sound on first hearing. The Church is necessary for salvation not because of its own merits, since it is a poor pilgrim, but because of God's actions through the Church, which exists because God wills it so. The necessity of the Church for salvation, then, has nothing to do with the human virtues of its members or even with a claim to the absolute truth of everything it has proclaimed throughout history—still less to the belief that it has never erred. The entire weight of the choice of the word "pilgrim" to describe the Church here makes it clear that it is a humanly provisional and erring community of faith that is necessary solely because God has chosen it, not because of its own merits. So, having issued their stern warning, the bishops use the remainder of section 14 to consider the situation of Catholics, who are those who are "fully incorporated into the society of the church . . . by the bonds of profession of faith, the sacraments, ecclesiastical government, and communion." They must persevere in charity and humility, recognizing that "their exalted condition results, not from their own merits, but from the grace of Christ." While, however, the call to a healthy humility on the part of individual Catholics is salutary, the language certainly suggests that membership in the Church gives the faithful an objectively "exalted condition" and returns us to a focus on being within the visible Church that is not at all, theologically, what the remainder of this section of *Lumen Gentium* seems to intend. In the tension between some elements of section 14 and the argument of sections 15–16 we encounter further unfinished business, business left undone perhaps by the need once again to satisfy both more traditionalist and more pastoral perspectives among the Council fathers.

Section 15 remains within the Christian community by considering the relationship of the Church to those "who are honored by the name of Christian, but who do not however profess the faith in its entirety or have not preserved unity of communion under the successor of Peter." The term "joined in many ways" is employed here to show the close links that exist, a list of doctrines and devotions that these "Churches or ecclesiastical communities" share with the Catholic Church is enumerated, and the section ends by expressing the desire for Christian unity "so that the sign of Christ may shine more brightly over the face of the Church." This final remark is particularly important, since it ties the desire for unity to the apostolic purpose of the Church, claiming, in effect, that the point of ecumenism is not the reclaiming of lost souls but the effectiveness of Christian mission beyond itself. The idea that other Christians are somehow personally disadvantaged in their quest for salvation is thus finally laid to rest here. The absence of Christian unity is fundamentally a structural problem that endangers Christian mission and says nothing at all about the virtue or holiness of members of other traditions.

At this point in their discussion the bishops appear to have over-looked or avoided one important consequence of their wonderful words about other Christians. To see the point, we need to recall our discussion of the relationship between baptism and mission in the second section of the book. There we saw that the baptismal priesthood, shared by all the faithful, is the basis for Christian mis-sion. It is because of baptism and its completion in confirmation that Christians are called to mission, and as the text clearly implies, the bulk of Christian mission beyond the Church is the work of the laity. Ordained ministers have as their primary responsibility the spiritual nourishment of all the faithful, while the laity spread the love of God in the world. But if this is so, then is it not true that all the baptized, Catholic or not, are engaged in the mission of the Church in the world?

The suggestion that Christian mission is the responsibility of *all* the baptized, not merely those baptized within the Roman Catholic communion, is replete with implications. Most obviously, it confirms (if confirmation were necessary) that the role of Christian mission is not primarily to increase the number of the baptized, still less the number of Catholics. Instead, we should think of Christian mission as any action that successfully increases the possibility that others may encounter the grace of God. For some, perhaps, that might be in a direct encounter with the Christian Gospel. But for far more it is likely to occur in the simple contact with people of goodness, "secular" lay Christians who live in the world and through who they are, what they say and do, and how they interact with others demonstrate that the world is the place in which a loving God cele-brates the growth of human love and solidarity.

A second implication of the realization that all Christians and not just Catholics are engaged in the mission of the Gospel is that the message of the vision of the last judgment in chapter 25 of Mat-thew's gospel has to be universalized, as the injunction to spread the love of God in the world must be concretized. Who are "the least of these my brethren" referred to by the Lord as those who "are" Christ for us, and whose basic human needs must be cared for if we are to be saved? Evidently, this refers to everyone in need if the Council fathers are right that everyone "belongs to or is related to" the people of God. So Christian mission begins, if it does not end, in care for the needy of whatever faith and those without faith. Thus, evangelization moves from being the Catholic concern to grow the (Catholic) Church to a very different picture: the work of all Christians to facilitate the universal human encounter with divine grace.

If the discussion of the place of various Christian communities relative to the Church is quite interesting, the ensuing consideration of non-Christian peoples in section 16 is breathtaking in its comprehensiveness. Here, we enter the realm of those who "have not yet accepted the Gospel" but who "are related to the people of God in various ways." The Jewish people are described as "beloved" and Muslims are applauded for their faith in the one God. "Nor is God remote from those who in shadows and images seek the unknown God," seemingly a reference to Hindus and Buddhists among others, and those who through no fault of their own do not know the Gospel but "seek God with a sincere heart" and "try in their actions to do his will as they know it through the dictates of their conscience"; they "may attain eternal salvation." Indeed, "the assistance necessary for salvation" is not denied to anyone who "not without grace, strive[s] to lead a good life."

Among the relatively few scriptural images that describe the community of faith are those of "the grain of mustard seed," "the leaven in the mass" (Matt 13:31-33), "the salt of the earth," and "the light of the world" (Matt 5:13-16), so the bishops' assertion that their claim for the necessity of the Church for salvation is drawn from "Scripture and tradition" must at least include these images. Indeed, the nature of our world today and the place of the Church within it suggest that we should give particularly close attention to leaven, mustard seed, salt, and light since they highlight the instrumentality of the Church or, to follow more correctly the words of Jesus, of the kingdom of God.[13] Jesus is constantly stressing that the kingdom of

---

[13] On this, see T. Howland Sanks, *Salt, Leaven and Light: The Community Called Church* (New York: Crossroad, 1997).

God is growing among us now, perhaps tiny or hidden, but that its fullness lies in God's future. Here and now, then, the importance of the Church does not lie in itself, but rather in its place in the divine plan. Consequently, its concern should be not for itself but for the world or the fullness of the kingdom for the sake of which it exists. If it must have any self-concern it can only be thus: is the Church faithful to its role as leaven, salt, and light? All three images make clear that the importance of the community of faith has nothing to do with any other kind of self-concern, and indeed that its work is that of something small that has an effect on something much bigger. A loaf of bread requires a lot of flour and very little yeast, and when you are making soup you have to be very careful not to overdo the salt.

There can be little doubt that as they constructed these sections of *Lumen Gentium* the Council fathers were deeply influenced by the thought of the Jesuit theologian Karl Rahner. Rahner had famously argued that because God wills the salvation of all and because the will of God can only be frustrated by the free choice of an individual, all people must somehow experience the offer of saving grace in their lives, if not as Christians then through their own religious traditions or through the anthropological constant that draws all human beings toward the light of truth. Rahner was also adamant that the offer of grace extended by God to all human beings was the saving grace of Christ's death and resurrection. Hence the Muslim or the Buddhist was brought into contact with saving grace through his or her own religious tradition, but it was the saving grace of Christ that they encountered there. Rahner believed that this formulation made it possible to give appropriate respect to all the world's great religions without abandoning the central Christian conviction that Christ is the one savior, and it is evident that the Council fathers were persuaded by his argument.

Lumen Gentium's discussion of the religious other and the relation of other traditions to the Catholic Church is both welcoming and firm. Its basic conviction that all people of goodwill either "belong, or are related," to the people of God, "this catholic unity which prefigures and promotes universal peace," is quite without the historic defensiveness of the Church. Gone is the us/them vision of the world of faith and the triumphalism born of insecurity that so typically accompanied it. Instead, we find a generous openness to a future in which the grace of God is at work in all hearts and the "catholic unity" that God wills is, if not viewed eschatologically, at least seen as a work of the ages. The Decree on Ecumenism (*Unitatis Redintegratio*) and the Declaration on the Relation of the Church to Non-Christian Religions (*Nostra Aetate*) only fill out this set of convictions in a way that has changed the ecumenical face of the Church forever and, perhaps, more than simple talk of *aggiornamento* may be the lasting result of the Council that would have been closest to the heart of John XXIII.

If we could fly up into the air and take a bird's-eye view of how the bishops understand the whole of the religious world, we would immediately say that the Council did not abandon the Church's claims to centrality, if not to superiority, in its role as sacrament of Christ in the world. It is clear that the bishops saw the world as a series of concentric circles and not as a pie chart of segments, each of which touches the point at the center. At the center of the economy of salvation stands the Catholic Church (in the view of the bishops), surrounded most immediately by the other Christian churches with those that are most like the Catholic Church in closest proximity (Orthodoxy, the Anglican Communion). Beyond the Christian churches come Judaism and Islam, followed by the nontheistic Eastern religions and lastly, but still "related to" the people of God, those who do not follow any religion but unbeknown to themselves "seek God with a sincere heart, and, moved by grace, try in their actions to do his will as they know it through the dictates of their conscience" (16). In the outer circles of this vision the agnostics and the Hindus are following their own consciences or their own venerable religious traditions and finding them a source of saving grace, *but only because these concentric circles are related in ways they do not know to the still point at the center*, without which there would presumably not be the one saving truth but many possibly incommensurable visions of salvation.

In the years since the Council there has been a great deal of ecumenical *rapprochement* and a considerable thawing in relations between Catholicism and other world religions, particularly Judaism. Neither, however, has been without its difficulties and on the Catholic side these problem areas can be traced in large part to ambiguities in the Council's treatment of ecumenical and interreligious dialogue. In ecumenism we have seen major dialogues especially with the Anglican Communion and with the Lutherans, with a growing understanding of questions of ministry and sacraments on the one hand, and of the meaning of justification on the other, but these developments have not led to any institutional movement forward. There has been no progress on intercommunion or on the recognition of the validity of one another's orders at the level of church organizations themselves. Rightly or wrongly, this is often considered to be because of reluctance or inertia on the part of the Catholic Church rather than the other dialogue partners. In the area of interreligious dialogue, the situation is both easier and more difficult. On the positive side, since Church unity is obviously not an objective, the heat is off when it comes to measuring the institutional implications of growing understanding. On the negative side, the Catholic Church cannot sidestep its conviction that there is one true Church, that this "subsists in" the Catholic Church, and that any suggestion that salvation in and through Christ may not be the way to think of the saving work of non-Christian religions is a serious error. On the ecumenical front, consequently, we see a shift away from talk of unity and its replacement by the rhetoric of "listening and learning."[14] In the area of interreligious dialogue there is a growing list of Catholic theologians who have incurred the displeasure of the papal magisterium by exploring more freely than the institution would like the question of how exactly salvation in Christ relates, if at all, to the grace of God discerned in non-Christian religions.

The vision of the Church's relationship to the people of God, and the way in which the bishops clearly speak of the Church as the center point to which all others are somehow related, should not be interpreted to mean that each individual Christian is somehow closer to God than his or her Buddhist or agnostic counterpart. Somehow we have to find a way to balance the sense that the Catholic Church has a central role and significance in the divine plan with the conviction that divine grace is universally available. It may indeed be that the Church is necessary for salvation, as the Council fathers insist, but that does not mean that salvation is encountered only through the agency of the Church. Indeed, salvation is a response to the offer of divine grace that comes somehow to each individual, and holiness is measured by the generosity of our response to God's self-giving, not by the moment we happen to occupy in history or the place in space and time. It is because God sees into human hearts that, ultimately, issues of our personal identity are irrelevant, and

---

[14] On this topic see especially *Receptive Ecumenism and the Call to Catholic Learning: Exploring a Way for Contemporary Ecumenism*, ed. Paul D. Murray (Oxford: Oxford University Press, 2008).

yet so much ecclesial and theological energy has been expended in making fine distinctions about the kind and quality of grace that is available to different persons.

All of these considerations of the universal availability of salvation have ecclesiological consequences. If this is God's work, then the Church's cooperation with the divine purpose must require much greater openness to the wisdom of the non-Christian world than has typically been the case. In the past, even those Christians who were open to people beyond the pale saw the Church's role essentially as militant, spreading the Gospel by drawing as many people as possible into the ecclesial communion. When today under the influence of Vatican II we see the Church more as a sacrament and a servant, and moreover passing through history as a pilgrim, the military metaphors are displaced by the more biblical images of leaven, salt, and light, which point the Church toward a new self-understanding as an instrument of a divine purpose in which the incorporation of others into the community of faith, however desirable, is not the objective of our apostolic activity. God's will for all people is that they be saved, not that they necessarily be baptized, and there is no necessary connection between the two.

Chapter 8

Who Is My Neighbor?

The Look of Surprise on the Face of the Saints

Because the grace of God is present in the world in ways that it is not present in the Church, an ecclesiology that takes seriously the vision of Vatican II outlined above will inevitably include reflection on what can be called "a theology of the world," if only because we need to ask the question "who are the saints?" and not the more direct but less polite, "so, who is in and who is out?" Elizabeth Johnson, in whose shadow anyone writing on this topic stands, has written that because "the communion of saints does not limit divine blessing to its own circle . . . it comprises all living persons of truth and love."[1] "Saints" populate the reign of God, not merely the Church. Indeed, the emerging reign of God is as wide as the world, if not the cosmos, and to consider "the saints" is immediately to engage the topic of Church and world or Church and reign of God. Most if not all Catholic Christians today naturally think of salvation being offered to all people, not merely to the baptized, or theists, or believers in "the transcendent." Most know that saints and sinners are present in Church and world alike. Even Augustine understood this, writing that "there are some whom God has whom the Church does not have, and some the Church has whom God does not have."[2] Such a perspective is in itself a strong check on ecclesial hubris of a more obvious kind, especially if we do not go on to make

[1] Elizabeth Johnson, *Friends of God and Prophets* (New York: Continuum, 1999), 220.
[2] St. Augustine, On Baptism, 5.27.38.

the mistake of thinking that we have a good idea who is in which group. We should all daily be chastened by the warning in Matthew 25 that the Last Judgment will be a day of great surprises.

One memorable version of an ecclesiology of eschatological surprise can be found in Flannery O'Connor's late story *Revelation*, doubtless familiar to many readers.[3] The outline is simple. Most of the story takes place in a rural doctor's waiting room where Mrs. Turpin, a farmer's wife, ruminates on the varieties of humankind around her and what she believes to be the good fortune that has placed her in a superior condition to all of them. Decent in a way, even generous, Mrs. Turpin is also narrow-minded and possessed of the casual bigotry whose modulations O'Connor captures perfectly. Her world is divided between the decent and respectable people who are remarkably like her and her kind, and everyone else. Her conversion, not too strong a word, is initiated when she is hit by a book titled *Human Development* hurled by a young epileptic named Mary Grace. Even O'Connor can be too obvious at times. Mrs. Turpin goes home, pondering in her heart the attack and the words that followed it as Mary Grace says to her, "Go back to the hell you came from, you old warthog!" Why was the book thrown at her and not at the white trash or the black people in the doctor's waiting room? How, she wonders, can she be both a warthog and yet saved? God answers her with a vision in the fields at sundown. She sees a host of individuals, "the saints," on the march toward heaven. But she is astonished by the fact that "her sort" of people are preceded by dancing bands of black folk, "white trash," lunatics, and others who cannot be classed as respectable. The "decent people" form the rear of the procession, "marching behind the others with great dignity, accountable as they had always been for good order and common sense and respectable behavior." They were the only ones who could sing on key, but "she could see by their shocked and altered faces even their virtues were being burned away." As the vision fades she returns to her house. "In the woods around her," concludes O'Connor, "the invisible cricket choruses had struck up, but what she heard were the voices of the souls climbing upward into the starry field and shouting hallelujah."

---

[3] Included in Flannery O'Connor's collection of stories, *Everything That Rises Must Converge* (New York: Farrar, Strauss & Giroux, 1965).

O'Connor's evidently purgatorial vision nicely combines the joy and the anguish that mark those on their way to heaven. The cleansing of their souls is a necessary step from the insecure possession of grace and truth that marks what tradition calls the Church militant to the pure joy and celebration of the Church triumphant. The proleptic joy of purgatory comes from the confidence of final possession of the vision of God, the anguish from "the refiner's fire" wielded by the messenger of the covenant in the book of the Prophet Malachi (3:2). Malachi may not have been familiar with purgatory but he hits the theological nail on the head; the cleansing is not some chronological stage of being prepared to meet God so much as the effect of encountering God as sinful people. The catalogue of social sins that Malachi lists as the subjects of judgment recalls us both to Matthew 25 and to Mrs. Turpin:

> Then I will draw near to you for judgment; I will be swift to bear witness against the sorcerers, against the adulterers, against those who swear falsely, against those who oppress the hired workers in their wages, the widow and the orphan, against those who thrust aside the alien, and do not fear me, says the LORD of hosts. (Mal 3:5)

We could reflect on this fairly standard list of prophetic denunciations to challenge the Church one more time to greater efforts on behalf of social justice, and it would not be unproductive to take that path. However, this time let us tread this well-worn path a little less directly and focus instead on the challenge to those "who thrust aside the alien." Any failure in humility leads to an act of exclusion. This was Mrs. Turpin's sin, and it may more commonly be that of our Church. The "virtues" of the respectable people that were, to their amazement, being burned away were those built on a world marked by a deep distinction between *us* and *them*, like the unthinkingly self-righteous publican who stood up front in the synagogue and prayed in thanks to God for his difference from other people. His sin was not his faithfulness to the law but his failure in solidarity, just as the poor man with whom he is unfavorably compared finds his salvation not in his virtue—which may in any case have been less than that of the publican—but in the absence of invidious comparisons with the other.[4] Behind O'Connor's story is another well-known and well-worn parable—the tale of the Good Samaritan. Mrs. Turpin is

---

[4] Luke 18:9-14.

learning the hard way the answer to the question with which that parable is introduced, one that is central to ecclesiology: "Who then is my neighbor?" How can we answer this question without ending up in an us/them kind of position where humility is all but preempted?

In the introduction to a collection of essays published in 2000, Archbishop Rowan Williams suggests "a threefold division into *celebratory, communicative* and *critical* styles" of theological reflection that is particularly useful in answering our question about humility and theological neighborliness.[5] The first or "celebratory" mode is that of hymnody or preaching, in which an effort is made to look at the "internal connections of thought and image" and so "to exhibit the fullest possible range of significance in the language used" (xiii). For all its value and beauty, this kind of reflection can become too wrapped up in itself and will benefit from a second mode—that of "communication" with other idioms and ways of thinking—with the intention of emerging from any "strange detour" more confident and stronger than before. Finally, there is a critical moment where theology enters into a reflexive critique of "its own inner tensions or irresolutions," which can certainly head in the direction of agnosticism but equally possibly toward "a rediscovery of the celebratory. . . . And the cycle begins again" (xv). Needless to say, these three ways of thinking theologically are not accomplished in isolation from one another; nor is any theologian exclusively engaged in one or two and not the third. But there is no doubt that different thinkers and even different churches lean one way or another. Williams identifies the Orthodox Church as a prime exemplar of the celebratory style, and it would not be going too far to suggest that Roman Catholic theology, at least today, might be more communicative, while classical Protestant thought's taste for dialectic leans it toward the critical mode. The emphases in *Gaudium et Spes* on reading the signs of the times and learning from the other certainly support this location of current Catholic theology.

O'Connor's *Revelation* has left us with an unforgettable image of how good people can fall into pride and presumption, and indeed of how a world structured by categories of *us* and *them*, whether or not that is a racial divide or some other set of categories, leads us into profound social and religious error. The consequences of the failure to know how to respond to the other are at the heart of Jesus' parable of the

---

[5] Rowan Williams, *On Christian Theology* (Oxford: Blackwell, 2000).

Good Samaritan. Forewarned by the sobering example of Mrs. Turpin and armed with Williams's three modes of theological inquiry, we can now turn to this famous story. The question to which the parable is a response is well-known—"Who then is my neighbor?"—but the answers it offers may be quite surprising.

Celebration: When the Saints Go Marching In

"Celebration," the first of Williams's three theological modes, occurs in theological reflection employed by the Church as it attends to the internal coherence of the tradition. Of its nature, it is upbeat and occasionally even self-congratulatory. From this perspective, whether it is the covenant community of Israel, communion in the blood of the Lord, communion in the body and blood of Christ on the altar, or communion in mission and witness to the Gospel, the implication is clear. We are a band of sisters and brothers united in faith and love. In the book of Leviticus God calls the whole community to holiness: "For I am the LORD your God; sanctify yourselves therefore, and be holy, for I am holy" (11:44). The New Testament takes up the same theme, "As he who called you is holy, be holy yourselves in all your conduct; for it is written, 'You shall be holy, for I am holy'" (1 Pet 1:15). God calls the covenant people of Israel, Jesus calls together his disciples, and from them the faithful people who will constitute the Church are called out from the multitude and called together for an apostolic purpose. The imperative to *be* holy is often overlooked, with the result that the Church's holiness can come to seem ontological. It is never our condition, always our task.

In both the Hebrew Bible and Christian New Testament, the holiness is in the calling, but the calling together as the people of God is for a purpose larger than the mere existence of the community itself.[6] Israel is called to be a light to the nations, as in Isaiah's words, "It is too light a thing that you should be my servant to raise up the tribes of Jacob and to restore the survivors of Israel; I will give you as a light to the nations, that my salvation may reach to the end of the earth" (49:6). And the Christian community of faith is described in

---

[6] On mission in the Hebrew Scriptures see Walter C. Kaiser, Jr., *Mission in the Old Testament: Israel as a Light to the Nations* (Grand Rapids, MI: Baker, 2000) and James Chukwuma Okoye, *Israel and the Nations: A Mission Theology of the Old Testament* (Maryknoll, NY: Orbis, 2006).

the Gospels as like a lamp on the lampstand, indeed "the light of the world" (Matt 5:14-15, Mark 4:21, Luke 8:16). The image of "light" is particularly helpful because it possesses both a centripetal and a centrifugal dimension. Light attracts, like moths to a flame, and light gives light to those who are in darkness. Both the mission of Israel and that of the Christian Church include drawing people to the covenant community or the communion of saints and going out into the world to shed the light. But none of these statements in themselves collapse the distinction between Church and world. The lamp gives light to those in darkness, the yeast—to use the other familiar analogy—raises the dough but it is not identical to the dough. The salt enhances the food but is not itself the food. And, of course, all three images remind us that the purpose to which the community is called is God's purpose, not ours. Light, yeast, and salt have themselves no inherent intentionality. God places the light, God adds yeast or salt to the recipe. The light is valueless unless there is something to which to give light, and yeast and salt alone are quite inedible.

When we see the Church as light, yeast or salt, we see the Church as the community of saints, in relationship to the world as needing light, leaven, or savor. Congar once wrote that Church and world are not to be imagined "like two crowned sovereigns looking sideways at one another as they sit on the same dais" but "much more like the Good Samaritan holding in his arms the half-dead man, whom he will not leave because he has been sent to help him."[7] In the theological moment of celebration, the identification of the Church with the Good Samaritan reaching out to the wounded victim is an important assertion of the priority of mission that draws attention to the fact that the Church throughout history has been a source of succor and consolation to suffering people, Catholic or not. In the Catholic tradition in particular, the many orders of religious women have always made an enormous contribution in the fields of nursing and education. Religious, both men and women, exercised a preferential option for the poor many centuries before the phrase was coined. Even today, Catholic Charities is the largest private network of social service organizations in the United States, much of their work being direct aid to the needy, Christian or not. Whether one

---

[7] From *The Wide World My Parish*, quoted in *Yves Congar: Essential Writings*, selected with an introduction by Paul Lakeland (Maryknoll, NY: Orbis, 2010), 64.

calls this work humanization, pre-evangelization, or preparation for the Gospel, it is an integral component of mission and witness without which the proclamation of the good news of Jesus Christ is incomplete. The underlying vision of the Church that supports this strong claim is evident in Scripture and tradition and, to refer us to Matthew again, evidently matters on the Day of Judgment.

The Parable of the Good Samaritan is appropriately used in this celebratory mode of reflection, but it must be employed with caution. It is quite pertinent to see the action of the Samaritan responding to the needs of the victim as an image of the ideal relationship of the Church to the world, provided we do not blind ourselves to other elements in the story. Above all, what are the ramifications of the fact that the Samaritan is an outcast from the people of Israel? And what exactly is implied by the evidently greater virtues he demonstrates than that of the two examples of Mrs. Turpin's respectable people, the priest and the Levite, who "pass by on the other side"? Moreover, has anyone considered the role played by the victim, especially as he begins his return to health and can reflect on all that happened to him? The Church as Good Samaritan embracing the world as the wounded victim must always bear in mind three disquieting questions: who is my neighbor, who is holy, and who is "the saint"? In the Gospel parable, Jesus is most definitely not reassuring his listeners about their own role but rather encouraging them to use their imaginations to discompose their own religious universe.

The problem with celebration is that it suffers from being undialectically centripetal. When we set out to take the lessons of the Good Samaritan to heart and see the Church as Congar suggested, even when we in some measure succeed in being that Church of compassion and service, we may be too focused on being the star of the soteriological show. Williams was thinking something like this when he pointed out that the theological language of celebration, though disciplined, is also vulnerable. Its weakness is that it becomes "sealed in on itself," writes Williams, so that the reflective process suffers "freezing" and the possibility of illuminating or modifying concrete historical situations is denied.[8] It is not that the celebratory language of intrachurch theological reflection is inappropriate in itself so much as that it can become locked in its own world, possessed of an essentially

---

[8] Williams, *On Christian Theology*, xiii.

self-referential hermeneutic that at worst is triumphalist and at best a sort of paternalistic vision in which the wisdom and the folly of the world alike are both subsumed in the totalizing explanation of faith. At this point some form of integrism threatens to emerge. Internally, this tendency toward the subsumption of the world under the umbrella of the ecclesial vision can be countered by greater attention to the Church's need for repentance, not only repentance before God as the sinners we are, but historical repentance before the world for all that we the Church have done in history to harm it, and all that we have failed to do to help heal it. But beware, for even when the theological language of celebration stresses its need for repentance, it can still remain centripetal, seeking the resources for repentance solely within the tradition, like a police force investigating its own corrupt officers. Too often the institutional response to the scandal of sex abuse has taken this form. In repentance, we bow down before God—the God who comes to us in sacramental life and grace-filled moments of Church life. Repentance also requires us to be open to the Spirit of God at work in the world. The world itself has wisdom and grace that we do not possess in the Church, and when in our sinfulness as a community of faith we can also be open to that grace and wisdom, theology will move into the second of Williams's three moments, that of communication, as we shall very shortly see.

The self-referentiality or centripetal tendencies of the Church are evident in ecclesial life today. They are the shadow side of the good that we do and the holy community that we are, but they follow clearly from an undialectical emphasis on celebration. In terms of the parable of the Good Samaritan, they are what happens when we rejoice in our identification with the model of concern for others and forget the disquieting context in which the parable is told. If we are the Good Samaritan who comes to the aid of the victim, then we are also the priest and Levite who is too busy about the "things of God" to be aware of the cries of the victim. And is it not just possible that some of our most loudly proclaimed teaching might suffer from the "freezing" that Williams mentions, as a consequence of which "the possibility of illuminating or modifying concrete historical situations is denied"?[9] Of course, what might seem to be frozen teaching to one person may be someone else's eternal truth, though the test has to be

[9] Ibid., xiv.

to determine if the teaching singularly fails to illuminate or modify concrete historical situations. The parable of the Good Samaritan is less a story about doing good than it is about breaking boundaries. The traditional orthodoxies of Judaism are challenged by the choice of a heretic, an unbeliever, an outcast from the covenant community as a model for emulation. Even more, the story insists that there *are* no boundaries to neighborliness. Love your neighbor as yourself is not about limits ("who is my neighbor?") but about the absence of limits ("Everyone!"). The lawyer, the priest, and the Levite work within the Law and want to know what it requires. Jesus teaches them to abandon it. The consequences of this parable for construing the right relationship between Church and world are thus considerable, and they are not exhausted by Congar's image of the Church as Samaritan embracing the victim.

Communication: In Search of Integrity

While the language of celebration can eschew the tendency toward a totalizing hermeneutic, its inevitably centripetal orientation means that it must be balanced by a more centrifugal consideration of its relationship to and its role in the world. This is the mode of communication. Theology as communication is close to but not identical with what is often described as "mediating theology." For Williams, the communicative moment reveals a theology that seeks "to persuade or commend, to witness to the gospel's capacity for being at home in more than one cultural environment, and to display enough confidence to believe that this gospel can be rediscovered at the end of a long and exotic detour through strange idioms and structures of thought." This kind of dialogue with an unfamiliar idiom is an act of confidence, assuming that it can help to "uncover aspects of the deposit of belief hitherto unexamined" and it must trust that the fundamental categories of belief are "robust enough to survive" this kind of treatment.[10] Its difference from mediating theology, it would seem, lies in its objective. Mediation is a species of apologetics whose objective is to speak to the other in words that can be understood, while communication is reciprocal, equally about learning from the other ways in which the doctrinal tradition itself can be enriched by the encounter. Mediation is frequently accused of adulterating the

[10] Ibid., xiv.

Gospel message in order to gain wider acceptance; communication in the sense we use it here is the opposite—namely, drawing on the other in order to strengthen the Church's grasp of its own beliefs.

In her "Hesitations Concerning Baptism," Simone Weil presents a challenging set of reflections on the presence of the Church in the world cast in the form of an explanation of why belief in God does not mean that she will necessarily seek to enter the Church. Weil writes that the fear she has for the Church is that it can too easily become an "us" over against the "them" of the world. "What frightens me," she wrote in January 1942, "is the Church as a social structure." She is "afraid of the Church patriotism which exists in Catholic circles," and which had led some saints wrongly to approve of the Crusades or the Inquisition. These saints "were blinded by something very powerful"—namely, "the Church seen as a social structure"—though Weil adds that she is only critical of "collective emotions." But of these emotions she writes very harshly, arguing that "the social is irremediably the domain of the devil. . . . The flesh impels us to say *me* and the devil impels us to say *us*." Of course she knows that the Church would not exist if it were not a social structure, but "in so far as it is a social structure, it belongs to the Prince of this World."[11]

Weil's challenge points to the dangers of the kind of ecclesial xenophobia that dogged the Church in the past, particularly in what John O'Malley calls the "long nineteenth century," stretching from the French Revolution to the eve of Vatican II.[12] There will be those of us who may think that she overstates the connection between the social and the demonic, but there is something chillingly accurate in her analysis of the way in which the language of "me" or "us" is almost inevitably exclusionary. It is hard not to see something like the *Syllabus of Errors* or the definition of papal infallibility at Vatican I, however formally correct they may have been in their times, as driven by a determination to assert the rightness of the Church over against the wrongness of the world. Where, indeed, in that whole long century is there any ecclesiastical humility in face of the world? And if after Vatican II we have largely got beyond the demonization of the religious other, it still remains true that when the Church uses

[11] Simone Weil, *Waiting on God* (New York: Harper & Row, 1951), 53–54.
[12] See O'Malley, *What Happened at Vatican II*, 53–92.

language like that in *Dominus Iesus,* or creates an "ordinariate" for conservative Anglicans fleeing their Church, however formally correct these may be, they do nothing whatsoever to draw the Church and the world closer together. Moreover, we need to recognize that if no lasting damage is done it is due to the forbearance of those who are not part of the Church, and not the generosity of those who are.

Weil was a secular Jewish intellectual deeply imbued with classical learning and whose grasp of Christianity seems quite deficient. For this reason, if for no other, she is an exemplar of how a "long and exotic" detour through the classics helps to enlighten the Christian tradition's grasp of its own story, particularly in her essay "Forms of the Implicit Love of God," where she leans heavily on the parable of the Good Samaritan. The story, she points out, tells us nothing about the life circumstances of either principal. We are consequently forced to attend only to their actions, to what Weil calls the supernatural virtue of the Samaritan and the capacity for supernatural virtue that the encounter with him has rendered possible for the victim.[13] While she characterizes justice in the classical tradition as "the even balance, an image of equal relations of strength," as a *supernatural* virtue justice "consists of behaving exactly as though there were equality when one is the stronger in an unequal relationship," and for the weaker one, "not believing that there really is equality of strength" and "recognizing that his treatment is due solely to the generosity of the other party."[14] The dialectic of generosity and gratitude in the story of the Good Samaritan mirrors the self-emptying of God in creation. The love of neighbor begins in creative attention to "a little piece of flesh, naked, inert and bleeding beside a ditch," but the attention is itself "a renunciation." When someone devotes her energy to giving life to another who will exist independently, she accepts diminishment.[15] The gift of life the Samaritan makes is a reenactment of God's act of creation and of Christ's passion and, as is surely evident from the language just used, of the woman who gives birth to a child. But like Christ and the new mother, the suffering and loss of self are more than compensated for by the new life that comes about.

---

[13] What follows here draws on Weil's analysis of "the love of our neighbor" in her long essay, "Forms of the Implicit Love of God," contained in *Waiting on God,* 137–215.

[14] Ibid., 143.

[15] Ibid., 146.

The picture Weil draws here has significant consequences for how we understand concupiscence and desire and gives definition to the embrace of the other in which Congar sees the paradigm for the relationship between Church and world. Weil contrasts the "natural justice of the Greeks," which undoubtedly disciplines desires but assumes that power is to be exercised to the "extreme limit of possibility," with the Christian vision in which it is the *restraint* of desire through which the human subject becomes a collaborator, a procreator in God's self-dispossessing work of creation. In other words, in the Christian vision I become powerful in my weakness. St. Paul in Philippians picks up this theme, for "though he was in the form of God," Christ "emptied himself, taking the form of a slave" (2:6-8). When the Samaritan embraces the victim he really loses something, just as the victim gains, and in the act of giving as losing, the Samaritan is divinized and the victim humanized. "In denying oneself," says Weil, "one becomes capable under God of establishing someone else by a creative affirmation," and this is "a redemptive act."[16] I lose and, miraculously, through losing I gain.

The supernatural virtue of love of neighbor, moreover, is the totally selfless act, only possible because it is God loving through us. To serve the other out of love for God is "misleading and equivocal," says Weil, and "the love of our neighbor is the love which comes down from God to man. It precedes that which rises from men to God."[17] There is only so much a human being can do and when we face a suffering victim and respond in love there can be no mediation, she thinks, not even the love of God. We the Church *are* the love of God for the world, we do not love the world because we love God. In other words in reaching out to the world there is a kind of forgetfulness of God. Indeed, in being the love of God for the world perhaps, in a way, we become like God in God's moment of self-emptying. Or we follow Jesus in the way of the cross, which amounts to much the same thing. God is the background that forms our humanity, we might say, not the foreground that gives shape to our praxis. For this reason if for no other, human solidarity in the praxis of justice takes priority over the adjudication of differences between faith claims. The last thing the suffering victim needs to know about the Samaritan is where he goes to church.

[16] Ibid., 147–48.
[17] Ibid., 150.

This picture has significant consequences for how we think of the Church's mission, not least because it suggests that we are most faithful to that mission when we are most forgetful of the reasons why we reach out to embrace the stranger, other than our common humanity. Our ecclesiology may suffer from the failure to see that our love of the world *is* our love of God and that our love of God *is* our love of the world. And yet there must be a difference, if Congar is right that the Church and the world are related to one another, "not like two crowned sovereigns looking sideways at one another as they sit on the same dais," but "much more like the Good Samaritan holding in his arms the half-dead man, whom he will not leave because he has been sent to help him." On the other hand and lest we think Congar is suggesting a smothering kind of embrace, there is also his warning quoted earlier that "final salvation will be achieved by a wonderful refloating of our earthly vessel, rather than by a transfer of the survivors to another ship wholly built by God." The Church and the world, then, are engaged in a collaborative venture in which the world, "our earthly vessel," will be "wonderfully refloated." They are not at loggerheads with one another; they are not enemies. They are not casting sidelong glances at one another but are locked in the embrace of Samaritan and victim.

Critique: "Nagging at Fundamental Meanings"

As important as the language of celebration and the role of communication with other ways of thinking, says Williams, is the moment of critique, where we engage in "nagging at fundamental meanings." How best can we nag at the fundamental meaning of "Church" or "all the saints"? And in the last analysis, doesn't it critically depend on what we mean by "all"? Perhaps it would be best to attend to the voices of at least some of those who have had to work harder to be included in the "all" that are "all the saints," people to whom our attention is drawn by the likes of Beth Johnson, Ada Maria Isasi-Diaz, Peter Phan, Shawn Copeland, Brian Massingale, and the many voices of liberation theology from Africa, Asia, and Latin America. Or we could turn to works of literature like the novels of Graham Greene or the short stories of André Dubus," or Gloria Naylor's unforgettable tale of sin and grace, *Bailey's Café*.[18] Collec-

---

[18] Gloria Naylor, *Bailey's Café* (New York: Vintage, 1993).

tively, theological reflection or works of the imagination that have their origins in the experience of difference or indeed in "strange detours" from religious pathways may have a lot to tell us about how "fundamental meanings" can be ways of locking people out.

One last look at the Good Samaritan starts us on our way. We saw that Congar wrote of the Good Samaritan embracing the wounded victim as an image of the Church/world relationship, and we have explored the value and some of the limits of that picture. But we have not so far noted that there is no particular reason to identify the Church with the Good Samaritan and the world with the wounded victim. Isn't it just as possible to turn things around? Indeed, might this not be an element in the paradoxical style of the parable and a good homiletic impulse on the part of Jesus? The point of the parable after all was not to teach the people to be good but to show them their narrowness of vision. While we have perhaps had some success in getting Jesus' point that "neighbor" knows no limits, we have not been as successful in recognizing that *we* may be the wounded person in need of the lesson of humanity provided by the outcast if we are to be restored to the full humanity we have somehow lost. When we move as a Church in grace, we are the Samaritan, but when we are full of sin, we are the wounded victim in need of succor. And when we are the wounded one, who is the Samaritan?

Because the grace of God is at work in the world in ways that the Church does not know and cannot control, our relationship to the world beyond the Church cannot simply be that of the Good Samaritan embracing the wounded victim. We are also the wounded victim silently beseeching the world beyond the Church for saving help. In our embrace of the world we are not healing the sinner so much as encountering the grace of God in unexpected places. We do not come to a richer humanity unilaterally but, rather, in dialogue with other sources of divine grace. When the Council fathers said that there is a real sense in which the Church must learn from the world, they meant that we need its help in order to be more fully the Church of God. As Charles Taylor has written, there are things the Church has learned from the world that it would not have discovered from its own resources.[19] If he is right, there is no reason to think that the

---

[19] James L. Heft, ed., *A Catholic Modernity: Charles Taylor's Marianist Award Lecture* (New York: Oxford, 1999), 16–18.

process has come to an end, though there seems to be little evidence in our Church today that we recognize even the possibility of worldly wisdom leading us to modify our traditional positions, especially in matters of social and sexual ethics.

There is another outsider in the Gospels, the Canaanite woman in Matthew,[20] whose extraordinary exchange with Jesus supports this understanding of the Good Samaritan parable in surprising fashion. The story is a familiar one, of the woman begging Jesus to heal her daughter and the rebuff to her, "I was sent only to the lost sheep of the house of Israel" (15:24). She entreats him further and in what must seem a perplexingly brutal response Jesus says that "It is not fair to take the children's food and throw it to the dogs" (15:26). Most people would leave at that point, but not her. Instead, she replies in kind, "Yes, Lord, yet even the dogs eat the crumbs that fall from their masters' table." Jesus is astonished, applauds her faith, and cures her daughter, and countless generations of homilists have preached about the depths of faith of this woman of no account. But if the woman of great faith is one focus of this story, the Jesus who had something to learn from her is undoubtedly another. Jesus is corrected by a non-Jew and a woman. Jesus learns something he did not previously understand. One can only wish that all our ecclesial encounters with the world beyond Christianity, and all the magisterial interventions in intrachurch issues, were as open to the wisdom of this unbeliever. A Jesus who has something to learn is a wonderful role model for those who teach in the name of Jesus, be they theologians or bishops.

A critical ecclesiology is one that takes seriously the limitations of the Church. That the Church exists not for itself but for the sake of the world, the saving mission that God has entrusted to the Church, is a given of contemporary ecclesiology. What is not always so clear is that, in being a sacramental community, it is at one and the same time positive and negative. It is the love of God for the world, and it is also in need of God's love for the world. It is God as present and God as absent. It is graced and sinful. It is the place of ordered desire and of disordered desire. It seeks integrity and falls short. It heals and it needs healing, it is the Good Samaritan embracing the victim and the victim embraced by the Good Samaritan. It is the Church

---

[20] Matthew 15:21-28.

that teaches and the Church that is always in need of being taught. As the sacrament of the love of God for the world in Christ, we bear the marks of the paschal mystery and those of God's self-emptying in the moment of creation. The Church as sacrament should not be preening itself nor abasing itself, but measuring its proclamation of the Gospel—itself a message of victory through failure—by the trinitarian and paschal insight that love costs. Because the world needs the Gospel as much as ever, it needs a Church that doesn't think it has all the answers but that is prepared to work in solidarity with others in the search for the truth that will set us all free—a Church that sees dialogue with our secular world as an encounter of grace with grace, sinners with sinners, and saints with saints.

Chapter 9

An Ecclesiology of Humility

History as Threat or Opportunity

As we have clearly seen throughout this book, the ecclesiology of *Lumen Gentium* supports in large measure a vision of the Church as a pilgrim people of God, and much of what is necessary in order to promote an ecclesiology of humility is already in place. Aside from the image of pilgrim, there are important resources in the renewed significance accorded to the sacrament of baptism and the theology of the baptismal priesthood that follow, in the recognition that God's saving grace is available to all people through their own traditions and religions, and in the importance given to the universal call to holiness. These directions are only strengthened, as we have seen, through more focused attention to one or another issue in the Decree on Ecumenism and the Declaration on Religious Freedom and the Declaration on non-Christian Religions, as well as the important opening to the world proclaimed in the Constitution on the Church in the World of Today. As a consequence, much of value has been achieved on the ecumenical front and in dialogue with other of the world's great religions. And yet, we have not come anything like as far as we might have hoped. Intercommunion among Christian churches is still stoutly resisted by the Catholic Church and though there are undoubtedly better relations with both other Abrahamic faiths and the great Asian religions, the institutional language through which they are often addressed, especially in the pontificate of Benedict XVI, is not helpful for bringing us any closer.

When we look for a reason why the Church's future seems not so settled as it once did, and when we recognize how much of the message of Vatican II has still not come to fruition, the answer is not hard to find. It lies in the persistent subcurrent of conciliar teaching and the way in which institutional Catholicism, for complicated reasons, has latched on to that to the detriment of *aggiornamento* in face of all that has happened in the Church and the world in the half century since the Council. The subcurrent is not simply the well-attested recalcitrance of the Roman Curia and its efforts to subvert the work of the Council. Rather, it is the traces of a theological outlook that the text incorporates but is simply out of tune with the overall theological perspective of the Council. While one can certainly have people of more conservative and more liberal temperament debating and struggling with the difficult task of reexpressing the faith for another time, one ought not to have directly competing theological voices actually at work within the conciliar documents. The particular standoff is not between those who favor more centralization or more devolution in Church authority, or even those who would like a more traditional or a less traditional liturgy. The central problem, rather, is that of history. There are places in the documents in general, and in *Lumen Gentium* in particular, where texts that ignore the element of historicity in tradition occur alongside those that recognize the doctrinal importance of historical method. Here, perhaps, is where the business of *Lumen Gentium* is most "unfinished." In the conflicts within the text we can see unresolved tensions within the Council itself. Addressing them then and there might have required more time (unlikely) or settling for somewhat less overwhelmingly positive votes for the finished documents (acceptable?). That this did not happen goes a long way toward explaining the high correlation between the problematic traces in the documents and the current state of the Roman Catholic Church—at least north of the equator.

Examples of the incompatibility of elements within the text are not hard to find. One is evident in the vision of the papacy carried over from Vatican I and the effort of the fathers to teach an understanding of episcopal collegiality that, at the very least, modifies the papal centrism of the earlier times. That Paul VI stymied the full application of episcopal collegiality by allowing the notorious *nota praevia explicativa* that undermined the bishops' authority is well-documented.[1] It has left us with a situation in which the

---

[1] See, for example O'Malley, *What Happened at Vatican II*, 244–45.

authority of the local bishop in his own diocese is firmly embedded in *Lumen Gentium* but the reality on the ground is that bishops have, if anything, less independence from Rome in matters of governance than they had before the Council. The balance between the global and the local church that Vatican II sought to express consequently became much more difficult to realize. The conservative forces that suppressed the forward movement of the Council on collegiality were and perhaps still are wedded to an understanding of the papacy that emerged initially at the beginning of the second millennium to insist on the independence of the Church from secular authority and that reached its apogee in the late nineteenth century as a defensive reaction against historical change. It is entirely possible that the weaknesses in today's Church are, in part, a product of resistance to change. Perhaps John Courtney Murray was right that the central significance of Vatican II could be found in its attention to the development of doctrine, and maybe institutional inertia diagnosed this and acted accordingly.

The clearest example in *Lumen Gentium* of the clash over the meaning of history is to be found in two passages that describe Jesus' role in establishing the Church, which we previously encountered in part 1 of this book. The first runs throughout the initial chapter of the constitution but is most succinctly expressed in section 5, where the fathers say that "the Lord Jesus inaugurated his Church by preaching the good news of the coming of the kingdom of God." After his death and resurrection, Jesus now "appeared as the Lord, Christ, and priest established for ever," pours out his Spirit, and:

> Henceforward the church, equipped with the gifts of its founder and faithfully observing his precepts of charity, humility and self-denial, receives the mission of proclaiming and establishing among all peoples the kingdom of Christ and of God, and is, on earth, the seed and the beginning of that kingdom. (LG 5)

Here, the Church grows out of resurrection and Pentecost, in the power of the Spirit, and "slowly grows to maturity." But compare this description to a second passage to be found in chapter 3 on the hierarchical nature of the Church:

> This holy synod, following in the steps of the first Vatican Council, with it teaches and declares that Jesus Christ, the eternal pastor, established the holy church by sending the apostles as he himself had been sent by the Father. . . . He willed that

their successors, the bishops, should be the shepherds in his church until the end of the world. In order that the episcopate itself, however, might be one and undivided he placed blessed Peter over the other apostles, and in him he set up a lasting and visible source and foundation of the unity both of faith and of communion. (LG 18)

More of the same follows, linking the establishment of the apostolic college to an event in the life of Jesus of Nazareth, stressing the close connection between the will of the apostles to have successors and the emergence of the office of bishop, and generally insisting on the present face of the Church as identical to that of the apostolic age: primacy of Peter, apostolic college, bishops as their successors, priests and deacons as aides to the bishop. Very little of this is historically discernible within the first-century Church, while the particular roles and responsibilities of pontiffs, bishops, priests, and deacons have been in constant process of historical change over the centuries.

In the years since the Council the Church has become greatly diversified in its current fortunes and in probable futures in different parts of the world, thus revealing the importance of a stress on the local church at exactly the time when the importance of the global church is more and more stressed. The churches of the South and of the North are parts of the same Roman Catholic communion but at very different stages of their development. In the South, the churches are growing in ways that those in the North experienced in centuries past, and to a high degree they are doing so in ways that reflect their cultures and ethos. In the North, rapidly contracting churches at the historic centers of Catholicism in Europe and, increasingly, in North America are dealing with an internal dialogue between those who would settle for a smaller and perhaps more "obedient" traditional Church and those who wish somehow to maintain the "Here comes everybody!" vision of Catholicism. They, too, are finding their way toward a Church that can accept the reality of a world of religious pluralism and continue to be of meaningful service, but they are attempting this in face of Roman centralism and the perspective of not a few bishops that continues to see secular humanism as a foe rather than an ally in humanization, and that finds competing visions of sexual and social ethics to be incompatible rather than mutually enriching. To be a Catholic Christian in North America today is to be torn between all that the traditions of the Church mean to us and all that we also inherit as children of our time in an honorably pluralistic society.

Robert Mickens, the distinguished Vatican correspondent of the London *Tablet*, describes the central problem we face as "the implosion of the Vatican."[2] In an age when absolute monarchies are a thing of the past and most if not all of us live in at least some kind of democracy, our Church is the one anachronistic holdout, insisting on maintaining a structure that is directly responsible for many if not most of our ills. Moreover, argues Mickens, the primary cause of inertia and opposition to structural change is clericalism, a phenomenon that seems to have succeeded in large measure in preventing the incremental structural change implicit in the Vatican Council in general and in *Lumen Gentium* in particular. Where are the structural changes that would make greater lay participation in the Church a reality? Where is genuine episcopal collegiality to be found? Whatever happened to the central image of the people of God?

Mickens has a deep knowledge of the inner workings of the Vatican and his judgment is surely accurate, though the issue of clericalism can be pursued in a little greater depth. Of course, clericalism is to a high degree a product of a mixture of the misplaced exercise of power and the fear of change, but its roots lie in the sin of pride. At the first session of Vatican II, the bishop of Bruges, Belgium, Emile de Smedt, criticized the first draft of the decree on the Church, then called *de Ecclesia*, for its triumphalism and clericalism. In doing so he evidently spoke for the majority of the Council fathers, and the final text of *Lumen Gentium* with which we are familiar has eradicated much if not all of both these characteristics. However, the way in which the Church has evolved in the half century since the Council does not show much evidence that the Vatican in particular took de Smedt's message to heart. The Vatican may be as out of touch with worldly ecclesial reality as Washington, DC, is with the lives of ordinary Americans. I wonder how much has changed since Congar wrote in his journal in October 1964 that "the Romans have a strange conception of things. For them, there are bishops and dioceses: these are *materia circa quam* [the matter about which], and there is 'the Church': that is, themselves, their authority, their administration, their legalism."[3]

---

[2] Robert Mickens "The Vatican's Implosion and American Catholics," *Ideastream* (November 16, 2012). See Mickens's address to the Cleveland Club in November 2012, available at www.ideastream.org/cityclub/entry/50405.

[3] Congar, *My Journal of the Council*, 606.

In this final chapter we will explore the question of what the Church would look like if it took seriously the need for more humility, and to suggest that the way forward may lie in correctly figuring the relationship between the centrifugal and centripetal impulses in the Church. These two terms are used loosely to indicate the Church's movement *out of* itself on the one hand, and its movement *into* itself on the other. Both of these have their legitimacy if we understand them to stand for mission in the first case and internal reform on the other. The hypothesis here is that failures in mission are a product of structural problems on the one hand, and on the other that the desirability of internal structural reform must be tested by one criterion alone: will the reform being considered lead to more effective proclamation of the Gospel broadly understood? Taking St. Irenaeus as our guide, the needed structural reforms will be those that make it more likely that the Church can contribute to the "glory of God"—that is, "the human being fully alive."

To structure the discussion we will make use of the four sets of reflections in the previous chapter: the challenge to self-righteousness, the proper exercise of what we might call "gospel confidence," the cost of service, and, finally, the Church's need of the world. All four impulses are grounded in the vision of Vatican II and in particular in how the Council fathers as a whole sought to imagine the Church in the text of *Lumen Gentium*. But it is not easy to see how any of the four can be accomplished within a Church that seems unable to escape clericalism and is apparently content to be an anachronism. Clericalism is essentially centripetal. Its exponents are narcissists. Its concern is for the perpetuation of itself, seemingly at any cost. The realities of the Gospel, the dynamic character of tradition, and the inescapability of historicity are alike ignored in favor of a model of ecclesial life that was invented less than two hundred years ago and has somehow been elevated to the status of hegemony. This hegemony, however, does not need to be overthrown in a revolution. The simple recourse to Gospel values will enable any one of us to proclaim that the emperor has no clothes.

How Not to Be Self-Righteous: "Decent People" and the Wretched of the Earth

When Mary Grace hits Mrs. Turpin over the head with *Human Development* and begins the process of self-questioning that ends with her celestial vision, Flannery O'Connor as good as lays out a program for Church reform. Her protagonist is not a bad woman, simply someone whose life has been lived within narrow cultural limitations that have led her to the belief that "decent people," meaning those like herself, are the worthy recipients of the favor of society and the beneficence of God. *They*, not we, are sinners. *They* need to get in line behind the good people; *they* need to learn to march in time and sing in tune. Somehow the bump on the head leads her to the realization that God's scale of values may not coincide entirely with her own. Those who can sing in tune do not, after all, merit a place at the front of the procession or a favored seat in the kingdom of God.

O'Connor is not writing about clericalism in the Church but about fallen humanity in general. Nevertheless, her point that narrowness of vision and the identification of righteousness with the respectable people are destined to be contradicted by another order of values not of this world is directly relevant to the situation in today's Church. Of course it would be foolish to suggest that all clerics are narrow-minded or that lots of lay people don't match Mrs. Turpin just as closely as many of the clergy. But the structural point remains, that when we have a Church built on an ontological divide even more stubborn than those of racism or ethnicity, we are almost guaranteed to be out of step with God. God who sees into the hearts of all human beings is not the least bit impressed by status or power. But those of us who are wedded to status or power are interposing human structures between ourselves and the reign of God. This is just as true for ecclesial structures as it is for the pompous posturing and self-centeredness that is evident in the higher echelons of society in general.

There are two ways in which Mrs. Turpin's experience has direct relevance to today's Church. The first has to do with the face the Church turns to all those who stand outside the boundaries of Christianity. As we have noted often in these pages, *Lumen Gentium* proposed a much closer relationship between all people and the Church than had previously been contemplated, saying indeed that everyone is somehow incorporated in or related to the people of God. However, Church practice at the highest structural levels has still to catch up with this vision, though the Catholic people in general seem to have progressed much further. Institutional considerations continue to use the language of objective defect or recognize the truth of other world religions only in those places where it seems to coincide with the Christian way of saying things. Any suggestion that God somehow communicates divine grace to those of other religions without benefit of the mediation of Christ is met with sanctions, as if the Church knows how God works.

The second lesson of O'Connors *Revelation* applies to internal issues in the Church. Compare, for example, the failure to address the plight of the countless thousands of Catholics who have joined the ranks of former Catholics out of real pain or simple disillusionment with matters like the lukewarm response to the scandal of sexual abuse or the extraordinary lengths to which Benedict XVI went to reconcile the traditionalist schismatics of the Society of St. Pius X to the Church.[4] On the one hand, those who are not finding spiritual nourishment in the Church are apparently written off in the hope that a smaller and "more faithful" Church will emerge, while those whose founding inspiration is the rejection of the latest general council of the Western Church are coaxed back into the fold as if their presence is more precious than those who have reluctantly departed for the welcome offered them by the Episcopal Church or the Unitarians. Is it irrelevant that the Society of St. Pius X is clericalist, while the vast majority of former Catholics are lay people? Isn't it just possible that the same clannishness that led to hiding the sex abuse scandal is at work in wanting all the clerics back together again?

What might be called the evangelical weakness of the Catholic Church today has to do with its stubbornly persistent clericalist self-understanding. Clericalism is, of its essence, exclusionary, and exclusion can never be part of the Gospel of Jesus Christ. It really is not possible for a Church built on structures of exclusion and holding a monopoly of power and control within the clerical 1 percent of its membership to proclaim effectively the Gospel of love and freedom. Mickens points to this in his own way by insisting that the ongoing commitment of Rome to an obsolete absolutist vision of a highly centralized Church constitutes its implosion. However, Rome alone is not the site of the problem. Across the northern hemisphere at the present day we can see part of the struggle for the future of world Catholicism being played out. The majority of commentators want to contrast the weak and failing Catholicism of the North with the

[4] Cindy Wooden, "Vatican Says It Is Willing to Be Patient with SSPX in Reconciliation Bid," *National Catholic Reporter* (October 29, 2012), http://ncronline.org/news/vatican/vatican-says-it-willing-be-patient-sspx-reconciliation-bid.

vibrant young churches of the South, but this seems to me to be a mistake, or at least too short-term a perspective. If, as successive recent papacies have insisted, democracy is the most desirable of political systems, at least for all except the Vatican City State, then as Christians we must surely be working to promote its growth. We cannot want to explain the health of Southern Hemisphere Catholicism by invoking the value of older, more authoritarian political systems. But one of the unavoidable social consequences of democracy is growing insistence on human and civil rights, also matters on which the Catholic Church has spoken positively on many occasions. So, when those states in which the Church is growing reach the desirable level at which one can proclaim their societies to be truly democratic, it would be highly unrealistic to imagine that the concern for personal rights will not spill over into the Church and precisely similar tensions emerge in the churches of Asia, Africa, and Latin America, as are currently in play north of the equator. Allowing for important cultural differences, many of the younger churches are in the place now where the churches of the North were a century ago. If human freedom and prosperity are legitimate values, their advent will lead to many of the same tensions in the years ahead that we face now.

What we are seeing occurring in the churches of North America and Europe is not just a crisis of internal structures or governance but a struggle to find a new way to be a truly missionary Gospel community. The growing weakness of these churches cannot be blamed on the lay faithful, who are either living out the passivity that older models of Catholicism assigned to them or struggling to find ways around a system that isn't working any longer. The failure of our Catholic Church in the North to be an effective witness to the Gospel must be laid at the feet of a leadership that is itself trapped in a structure not of its own devising, but which it has inherited, with which it is comfortable, and about which it apparently does not have the imagination to think creatively into the future. Recall once again that it is the primary pedagogical mistake of poor teachers to blame anyone but themselves when "it" just isn't working. If our efforts to proclaim the Gospel are not succeeding it is far more likely to be because we are using very poor methods or because we aren't actually preaching the full Gospel than because people have hardened their hearts. Good teachers go back to the drawing board. When this doesn't happen, we get what we have now. Older understandings of ministry as the preserve of clergy and religious are under severe stress, challenged both by newer forms of ministry, often lay, and questions that will not go away about the possibility of more flexibility in understanding who can and who cannot be ordained ministers. The resultant loss of credibility explains to a high degree our failure to arouse much interest at all among the young and the growing numbers of people who turn away for the greater nourishment they find in other churches.

The connection between these thoughts and the larger issue of an ecclesiology of humility lies in the way in which we understand the Catholic voice in today's world. Hopefully, the message of the Gospel has not changed over the millennia, but the world in which it must be proclaimed certainly has, and perhaps more in the last hundred years than in all the preceding Christian centuries. While the Council fathers seem in large part to have understood this, the Church in the half century since Vatican II has not. Here indeed is where there truly is a difference between the churches of the North and of the South. In Europe and North America where the challenge is largely to be heard in a secular society the temptation is to continue to think of Roman Catholicism as the only show in town, the beacon of truth in a heedlessly materialistic world. The Asian churches, on the contrary, know the reality of being a tiny minority in the midst of ancient world religions, Africa contends with the vitality of Islam, and Latin American Catholicism has to struggle with Pentecostalism. But all the members of all our churches, North and South, must face the challenge that Archbishop Rowan Williams pronounced when he spoke to the Roman synod of bishops in 2012: if we are not careful we will "run the risk of trying to sustain faith on the basis of an un-transformed set of human habits—with the all too familiar result that the Church comes to look unhappily like so many purely human institutions, anxious, busy, competitive and controlling." I must call on the Holy Spirit, Williams said to the assembled bishops, "to enter my spirit and bring the clarity I need to see where I am in slavery to cravings and fantasies and to give me patience and stillness as God's light and love penetrate my inner life."[5]

The archbishop's words suggest an insight or two that he might not have intended or might have been too polite to utter. Among the

---

[5] Williams, "Archbishop's Address to the Synod of Bishops in Rome" *Archbishop of Canterbury* (October 10, 2012), http://www.archbishopofcanterbury.org/articles .php/2645/.

"cravings and fantasies" that can afflict both individuals and communities are those of attachment to the familiar, and then our "untransformed set of human habits" fails to allow the truth of the Gospel to shine through the fallible human community. For Roman Catholics, lay and clergy alike, the Church as we have known it can be such a source of attachment, with the consequence that the Gospel may be more frustrated than proclaimed. Williams proposed that the best way to promote more effective evangelization is to foster the practice of contemplation, "to learn to look to God without regard to my own instant satisfaction," through which we will encounter "the key to the essence of a renewed humanity that is capable of seeing the world and other subjects in the world with freedom—freedom from self-oriented, acquisitive habits and the distorted understanding that comes from them." If I may translate this for the purposes of Catholic ecclesiology and, of course, absolve Williams from any intention to make this point, "when we confront the need to be an evangelical, missionary community we must recognize that the structures are there to serve the gospel and the gospel is not to be constrained by any structure, however apparently sacrosanct."

Effective evangelization as the centrifugal or missionary impulse of the Church requires healthy internal church life, thus the need for periodic centripetal activity to reform ecclesial structures or liturgy. A Church whose current life is built on the prideful distinction between laity and clergy, both in terms of decision making in the Church and liturgical roles, is highly unlikely to be a credible herald of the Gospel that precisely seeks to confound such an exercise of power or the practice of exclusion. The centripetal must serve the centrifugal. The resources for a return to healthy ecclesiality are right before our eyes: renewed attention to the Scriptures and the practice of contemplation advocated by Williams in that same, very significant address to the Catholic bishops gathered at the Rome synod in the fall of 2012. The possibility of finding the courage and the imagination for the necessary reforms in the service of reviving the mission of the Church lies in rediscovering the practice of humility. One dramatic way to recognize this would be to learn from the interiority promoted in the wisdom of ancient Asian religions. One indication of how far we may have to go to achieve this can be found in the persistent institutional suspicion of those who advocate such a path.

And so we return to poor Mrs. Turpin, nursing the bump on her head and receiving a vision in which all her assumptions about

God's scale of values are turned upside down. As we approach the heavenly kingdom, she is learning with a mixture of consternation and awe what *we* imagine to be the right order of things is just that, our fallible understanding based on our natural inclination to see ourselves at the center of the world. For Mrs. Turpin the revelation is that the wretched of the earth, the blacks and the poor whites, may be further along on the way to God than she and her respectable kinfolk. If O'Connor offers us a reason why, it is surely that living our life judging others puts us at the back of the queue for the kingdom. While our Church today may no longer be making quite that mistake about the poor and the suffering, it continues to see the wisdom of other traditions as valuable only insofar as it conforms to that of the Christian vision. It seems that there is no truth in other traditions that we can receive as revelation. Aside from making the grave mistake of assuming that those paths to wisdom that we designate "defective" are thereby so classified in the divine mind, we are also replicating Mrs. Turpin's mistake. The wisdom and grace of God is so much bigger than our petty human understanding. It may be that the great surprise for the institutional vision of Catholicism will come when on the day of judgment we see, ahead of us in line, Jews and Buddhists and Hindus and Muslims and any and every person who recognizes that the wisdom of God passes all human understanding. What, indeed, would the Church's missionary effectiveness be if that were the message we placed in the foreground?

How to Proclaim the Gospel Fearlessly: Holy Church, Holy World

Jesus' parable of the Good Samaritan provides us with a spectacular example of how proclamation and humility go hand in hand (Luke 10:25-37). The story, in response to the question "Who then is my neighbor?" is one of considerable complexity. The one who questions Jesus is clearly looking to limit the category of neighbor, since Jesus has just told him to love his neighbor "like himself." But the story invites the opposite conclusion. First, it clearly indicates that our neighbor is anyone with whom we come into contact who is in need. This should be lesson enough for anyone who wants to practice philanthropy on a smaller stage. Further, however, we have to note that Jesus' choice of the despised heretical Samaritan as the one who shows the pious Jew what it means to love one's neighbor is surely no accident. If the victim expands the concept of neighbor, the Samaritan explodes the audience's conception of who might be a teacher. But for now let us focus on the first and most obvious lesson that the parable teaches—namely, that the concept of neighbor knows no boundaries.

The Good Samaritan presents us with Jesus' ideal of how we should live in the world, attuned to the needs of those we encounter and generous in our response to them. The inclusion of the priest and the Levite as examples of people who fail on both counts is not meant as an attack on religious professionals and shouldn't be used to take cheap shots at today's clerics. Any one of us, lay or clergy, could be guilty of this kind of failure. Rather, it is the simple observation—emphasized by the choice of the Samaritan as the model—that virtue can be found anywhere, even in the most unexpected places. The grace of God, Jesus seems to be saying, is no respecter of places or persons. For that reason, as was hinted in the previous chapter, using this story to aggrandize our Church is fraught with peril. So long as we treat the parable as a call to a level of conduct that we do not always live up to, we are safe with the parable. The moment we begin to see it as a description of how the Church addresses human needs, triumphalism is lurking around the next bend.

If we have to approach the message of the parable of the Good Samaritan with humility and circumspection, it is also true that the Church's call to proclaim the Gospel and to do so fearlessly receives support and direction from the story Jesus tells. If we imagine ourselves in the place of the Samaritan, however provisionally, a number of important pastoral lessons stare us in the face. In the first place, the object of our concern is not this kind of person or that kind of person, but simply the one we encounter who is in need. The important detail about the victim in the story is not that he has been beaten by robbers and stripped and left for dead, but that he is helpless, and helplessness can take many forms. Then there is the priest and the Levite who pass by on the other side, who stand for the persistent human inclination to choose those whom we plan to help, rather than to let the needs of the world choose us.

The Cost of Service:
Kenosis *in* the Church, Kenosis *of* the Church

One of the lessons of Weil's reflections on the interactions between the Good Samaritan and the victim illuminates what Dietrich

Bonhoeffer memorably called "the cost of discipleship." When we truly give, Weil reflected, we transfer something from and of ourselves to the victim, and in doing so we are somehow diminished. In this exchange we mirror the saving action of God in Christ who "emptied himself, taking the form of a slave, being born in human likeness" (Phil 2:7). Christ's gift of self restores the human race to the possibility of full humanity in a renewed sense of our relationship to our Creator God. Any act of self-giving on the part of any human being recapitulates that saving action. As we give possibility to others we die to self, at least a little. But the Christian story also insists that in that death to self lies the way to new life. Beyond self-giving lies the restorative embrace of the divine.

Perhaps the most positive aspect of the language of "the new evangelization" that is current in today's Catholic Church is that it places the Church in the role of Samaritan and not like the scribe and Levite passing by on the other side. These religious professionals wrap themselves in their religious self-sufficiency and see no need to give. Their entry into new life, sad though it is to say, will have to wait for the event that opens them up to the dialectic of giving and receiving that the parable lays out. Perhaps they will listen and learn from the parable. Or perhaps they will experience victim-hood themselves and learn the hard way from the generosity of the other. As Weil commented, when the Samaritan is diminished by his generosity the victim is restored to humanity. The victim needs what the Samaritan has to give, but in giving what he has to give the Samaritan is also brought to a place of renewed life. The one receives, the other gives, but both grow in their common humanity.

The potential weakness in the turn to evangelization is that the Church may tend to see itself undialectically in the place of the Samaritan and not in that of the victim. As our earlier reflections in this chapter have shown, we are both simultaneously. Charged to proclaim the message of the Gospel, we hopefully can do so in such a way that we truly give ourselves to the task and do not just say the words. But the message of the Gospel we are called to proclaim is also a message for us, which we receive as sinners in need of grace. We are both the Good Samaritan and the victim in need of help. We proclaim and embody the grace of God as we also stand in need of that same grace. The parable tells us to look for that grace in some unexpected quarters, to learn from the love of God that suffuses the world, even the world that does not value the Church.

The ecclesiology that can encompass this spiritual insight about giving and receiving is one with which the Roman Catholic Church is not familiar. It has grown accustomed over many centuries now to being the most powerful Christian community in the world, often enmeshed with state power, but even when not so situated, theologically attuned to proclaiming its status as the one true Church. *Lumen Gentium*, as we saw much earlier in this book, finessed this claim in a moderate but still significant way by preferring to say that the one true Church of Christ "subsists in" the Roman Catholic Church. Thus the door was cracked open just a little for a more generous interpretation of the roles of other Christian traditions, though the Council never relented in its conviction that while other churches contained much of value they did so to the degree that their vision coincided with that of Roman Catholicism. Even after Vatican II, it would seem, the message is that there was nothing to learn *theologically* from other Christians, though this does not mean of course that we cannot learn morally from the virtuous other or, indeed, that they may not be examples of Christian living that can put us Catholics to shame.

The incompleteness of *Lumen Gentium*'s ecclesiological vision means that the Roman Catholic Church is ill-prepared to face its declining fortunes in the world north of the equator. The Church remains the largest single Christian tradition by far, and even in Europe and North America continues to have considerable influence. But this influence is waning along with the health of Church life. To focus just on the United States, one must wonder what are the long-term prospects for a Church in which active involvement in liturgical life is declining rapidly, in which older generations are far more participatory than the younger, and in which the influx of immigrants is hiding the catastrophic decline among those ethnic groups that were for so long the backbone of American Catholicism? The Irish, the Italian, the Poles, and the Germans are far more likely these days to be spending their Sunday mornings cheering for their children on the soccer field than shepherding them to church.

In his address to the synod of bishops, Williams suggested that "the new evangelization" should only be attempted in a profoundly ecumenical context. This challenge nicely situates the predicament of American Catholicism today. If we are to reevangelize our fellow citizens, and perhaps especially the young among them, it cannot be done by returning to familiar claims of superiority over other traditions, of isolation from other traditions, and of insistence on ethical positions that not only seem outmoded to younger Americans but may, in fact, be sources of scandal. Somehow or other, if the new evangelization is to work, the spirit and fruits of the Gospel of love have to be disconnected from the idea that gay people should live lonely lives or that condoms are not an appropriate means of reducing the spread of AIDS or HIV. To confuse time-conditioned ethical positions with eternal Gospel truths is to court further disaster.

One way to get beyond the present Catholic predicament of blunting the value of our religious tradition by surrounding it with inessentials is to learn from the example of other Christian traditions, in other words to become good ecumenical students. In terms of the dialectic of caregiver and victim in the parable of the Good Samaritan, it may be that the Roman Catholic Church has become the victim of the many centuries of its own success, success in which the enormous good that it has done has seduced it into believing that there is nothing to learn. The recovery of a healthy presence in the developed world may be a matter of standing down from the sense of religious superiority and placing ourselves firmly and equitably in the ranks of the many Christian churches, all of us at one and the same time bearers of revealed truth and yet incomplete and sinful institutions, needing one another for our completeness.

In Europe, where the situation of the Roman Catholic Church is far more parlous than it currently is in the United States, ecclesiology has moved closer to an appropriately humble posture. In the Netherlands in particular there are serious efforts to think about the shape of what they are not afraid to call "a new Catholic Church . . . emerging in the West."[6] Perhaps, then, before we open ourselves to the wisdom of other Christian traditions or that of the great world religions, we could begin at home and consider how we might be helped by our fellow Catholics who have the courage and wisdom to ask the questions that we in North America have not yet arrived at. The renovation of evangelization is not just about the message; it is also about the messenger, and the messenger is on the brink of radical change, not only within the churches of the Northern

---

[6] I am enormously indebted in the concluding sections of this book to a collection of essays published by the University of Tilburg, *Towards a New Catholic Church in Advanced Modernity: Transformations, Visions, Tensions*, ed. Staf Hellemans and Jozef Wissink (Zürich and Berlin: LIT, 2012). This quotation is from p. 7.

Hemisphere, where something between radical medical interventions and life support seems to be called for, but also and equally south of the equator, where vigorous but vastly different cultural forms of Catholicism are emerging.

Staf Hellemans has charted the course of the European Church from "ultramontane mass Catholicism" to "choice Catholicism."[7] Hellemans first suggests that new forms of religion, a variety of options, and the decline in social constraints mean that "commitment to an institutionalized religion is being considered as a non-evident act of choice."[8] Second, says Hellemans, we are moving toward becoming a minority church "without enforcing power," and while the minority status is surely truer for Europe than for the United States, the absence of enforcing power is common to both contexts. Church participation having become a matter of choice "with a very attractive exit-option" means, he thinks, that "the power-balance has shifted in favor of the laity," and this "makes the Church into a service organization that has to cater to a clientele that is conscious that it can always turn its head away."[9] So how should the Church adjust? Should it lower or raise its demands, appealing to lukewarm liberals or to the minority of committed believers? Should it engage modernity or should it stand out as a countercultural voice? These and other options are all on the table at this moment in history.

Hellemans depicts Catholicism today as a "religionized religion"— that is, it is no longer the total institution that it was in the day of ultramontane mass Catholicism. Today it is up to the believer to find ways to link the religion to the social forms of a pluralistic and often highly secular society. In the future the Church "will have to base its appeal almost solely on religious grounds." And so there arises the question of relevance: "How can the Church penetrate society as a religionized church?"[10] Given that it is a real question whether or not sufficient people are still interested in what the Church has to say and that it has to present its proposals in the open market of ideas, Hellemans is not optimistic that the former role of the Church can

[7] Staf Hellemans, "Tracking the New Shape of the Catholic Church in the West," in *Towards a New Catholic Church in Advanced Modernity*, 19–50.

[8] Ibid., 26.

[9] Ibid., 28.

[10] Ibid., 34.

be reclaimed and so concludes that "a more modest role in advanced modernity looks inevitable."[11]

In exploring the options for a more modest role for Catholicism Hellemans rejects that of becoming a sect (the conservative direction) or a fellowship (the liberal option) in favor of the status of being "a major minority church," that is, a religious group within a secularized society that retains "a substantial membership and a tangible influence."[12] Such a church will have to "attract and seduce people into its realm" and do so "with religious means only." There are four conditions for achieving this status. There must be new paths in devotion and spirituality. There must be a new "layered" tone to the Church's teaching and preaching that recognizes the variety of levels of commitment of those whom it wishes to reach. It must bring in new members, especially among the young and should reach out through greatly expanded use of media. And it must find a way to reform its structures so that there will be more transparency, more decentralization, and "more humility on the part of the institution."[13]

The Church in Need of Grace: Learning from the Other

If the larger challenge to Roman Catholic ecclesiology today is to see a way to be humble in face of the wisdom of other great world religions, both interreligious dialogue and receptive ecumenism make essentially the same demands on the resources of our theological tradition. For all its wisdom the Second Vatican Council did not adequately explore how its new openness to the world was connected to the mystery of grace, and *Lumen Gentium* in particular came up against a barrier it could not or would not cross when it pronounced all humanity to be somehow "incorporated in or related to" the people of God. Surely Rahner was hinting at something more than the vision of concentric circles with the Roman Catholic Church at the center when he opined that these words imply "the possibility of a properly salvific revelation-faith even beyond the Christian revelatory word." But how are we able to be open to wisdom that is *not* contained in the Christian tradition while continuing to assert the centrality of the Church in God's will to save the world?

[11] Ibid., 36.
[12] Ibid., 39.
[13] Ibid., 43.

One way to move forward toward the necessary humility without abandoning Christian faith is to reflect on the implications of the two opening assertions of *Lumen Gentium*, that "Christ is the light of the nations" and that "the church, in Christ, is a sacrament—a sign and instrument, that is, of communion with God and of the unity of the entire human race" (1). We are immediately made aware by the Council fathers that it is Christ, not the Church, that should always be the center of our attention, and that only with this firmly in mind can we then go on to see the essential but inevitably instrumental role that the Church plays in the economy of salvation. There are two important consequences of the bishops' choice of the model of "sacrament" to describe this instrumentality. One, familiar to all, is that a sacrament does not only point to what it signifies but also, in some way, already embodies it. The other is the dual meaning of sacrament as ritual (*sacramentum*) and as mystery of revelation (*mysterion*).

The Eucharist is the perfect example of how a sacrament both indicates and performs, in this case the union of believers with God in Christ. However, while sacramental rituals contain both these significatory and performative aspects, the looser and yet more profound use of the idea of sacrament to refer to the Church itself has to be seen in a slightly different way. The Eucharist is always the Eucharist, as long as the ritual is performed in the community of faith, and so long as this happens then the Church itself is sacramental to a degree. But because the reality of the Church exceeds the sacramental rituals, its performativity is a matter of degree. If we in the Church are unfaithful to the Gospel, then the sacramentality of the Church is to that degree diminished, though not entirely impaired. The sinfulness of Christians cannot but impede the clarity with which the Church serves as a sign of God's love for the world.

While it was only in the third century that theologians Origen and Tertullian used the term "mystery" (*mysterion* and *sacramentum*) to refer to the sacraments of the Church, it had for long been employed to describe the mystery of God's self-communication in history, which is indeed the fundamental meaning on which that of the sacramental rituals must depend.[14] The rituals are moments in the life of the Church and of the individual believer when God's grace (that is, God's self-communication) is particularly evident, but they would

---

[14] See, for example, Ephesians 3:1-12, where Paul receives the revelation of the mystery of the Gentiles' inclusion in God's plan. See also Colossians 1:24-29.

have no meaning if the grace of God did not, in fact, already and from all eternity, suffuse the earth. The mystery of God's salvific will is revealed in both Hebrew and Christian Scripture of course, but for Christians in a special way in the encounter with God in the person of Jesus Christ. Christ is himself often spoken of in contemporary theology as the sacrament of the encounter with God, and the Church in its turn is seen as the sacrament of the presence of Christ.[15] The Church points to Christ and makes him present in the world today, while Christ himself points to and makes present the grace of God.

We can then say that the reality of the Church as sacrament is embedded in the deeper mystery of God's offer of salvation to all, and this should cause us to pause. Within the Church we can speak with confidence of the way in which the sacraments are ritualized expressions of this greater mystery, but of the depths of this mystery itself we would be wise to maintain a prudent silence. Unfortunately, the Church is not immune to theological *hubris*, nor indeed to a vision of salvation that is overly ecclesiocentric. The Council fathers implicitly cautioned against these vices in their careful statement that the one Church of Christ "subsists in" the Catholic Church and in the way in which they claimed that it is "the Church" and not membership in it that is "necessary for salvation."

When we place the Church as sacrament in the context of the divine mystery, we become aware of a further important dimension that, while it points to the mystery of grace and to a degree embodies it, the sacrament does not exhaust the mystery of grace. While the Church points always beyond itself to the incarnate Christ, the very idea of sacramentality means that the world points always beyond itself to God its creator. To borrow some phrases from the work of Juan Luis Segundo, the realm of grace is "the community of redemption," which is the entire world, not only "the community of revelation," which is the Church.[16] God's salvific relationship to the whole created order is proclaimed by the Church, but its reality far exceeds it. If it were not so, then outside the Church there would be no salvation.

---

[15] These phrases are primarily associated with the work of Edward Schillebeeckx. See especially his *Church: The Human Story of God* (New York: Crossroad, 1993), 102–86.

[16] Juan Luis Segundo, *Theology for Artisans of a New Humanity: The Community Called Church*, vol. 1 (Maryknoll, NY: Orbis, 1973), esp. 98–112.

Such a humbler ecclesiology ought, for consistency's sake, to result in a more humble Church. If the Church is indeed God's instrument, that does not mean that its members are God's elect. We are, rather, servants of the will of God that the world be saved, in service to the glory of God that is the human being fully alive. In this task both individual Christians and the entire Church itself stretches out beyond itself into the world and, lo and behold, finds there God's grace awaiting it in people and places that we encounter. The Church's mission is not to *give* grace, as if it were pouring water on a parched land, but to meet grace with grace in an embrace that pours grace on a fertile land, while at the same time the Church drinks from the wells that it encounters there. As in the parable of the Good Samaritan, the Church is both giver and receiver. In giving and receiving, the Church plays its part as an instrument of the mystery of divine grace—a mystery that even the Church itself cannot fully comprehend.

Afterword

In the Age of Pope Francis

This book ends with a heartfelt plea for a humbler Church, and there is no doubt that in the early days and weeks of the pontificate of Pope Francis many of his remarks and gestures portended such a change. How the pontificate will work out, what its achievements and its failures will be, no one knows at this point and only someone even more foolish than the present writer would hazard to guess. And yet it would be a mistake to pretend that nothing has happened. Any new pope brings his own style and priorities to the table, and any conclave is a moment of anticipation for all Catholics, liberal and conservative alike. But rather than guess about the future and knowing how uncertain another path will be, there may be things to learn from a glance back at the kind of priorities that were dear to the heart of Cardinal Jorge Mario Bergoglio. It would no doubt be a mistake to imagine that he would leave those entirely behind as he becomes bishop of Rome, though the Latin flavor of his world will surely have to make space for a more global perspective. What we should expect to find consistent will be his focus on the poor, on making their concerns and their world the center of the church's priorities, together with his critique of self-referentiality, both ecclesiastical narcissism in general and clericalism in particular. It seems like both the bishop's palace and the stock market will be displaced by the stable at Bethlehem, and this can only be a good thing.

Index

Habermas, Jürgen, 105
Hahnenberg, Edward P., 83
Hebblethwaite, Peter, 19n7
Hellemans, Staf, 48n25, 148–51
Hopkins, Gerard Manley, 7
Humani Generis, xvii, xxx
humility, ecclesial, 103–26, 134–54
Hunter, James Davison, 46–54

Irenaeus, St., 80

Jesus Christ, 50–53, 78
John XXIII, Pope, xxx, 19–21
John Paul I, Pope, 23
John Paul II, Pope, xxv, 16, 17–18,
    80, 85
    and collegiality, 24–33
Johnson, Elizabeth, 118

Kasper, Walter Cardinal, xxv
Kaveny, Cathleen, 77
Kennedy, President John F., 39
Knox, Ronald, 108
Komonchak, Joseph, xvi, xxvii
    n24, 19n5, 23n11
König, Franz Cardinal, 18, 23
Kuhn, Thomas, xx
Küng, Hans, 17–18

Lafont, Ghislain, 77, 80–82
laity, xxxi–xxxii, 5, 61–99
    as ecclesial ministers, 88–99
    cooperation with ordained
        ministers, 68–70
    mission and ministry, 70–73
    secularity of, 64–67
lay ecclesial ministry, 88–99
Leo XIII, Pope, xxvii
Lercaro, Giacomo Cardinal, 20
Le Saulchoir, xxx
Lonergan, Bernard, xvii–xxi, 85–86

Mannion, Gerard, 32–33, 104–7
Metz, Johann Baptist, xxi
Mickens, Robert, 138, 141

Morris, Bishop William, 16
Murray, John Courtney, xvii,
    xxiv–xxviii
Murray, Paul D., 116n14

Oakley, Francis, 14n6
O'Connor, Flannery, 104, 119–20,
    140–41, 145
O'Malley, John, 15n7, 127
Origen, 152
Ottaviani, Alfredo Cardinal, xvii, 3

Paul VI, Pope, xxv, 19–21, 135
periti, 5–7
Philips, Gérard, xxxi
Pius X, Pope, 55
Pius XII, Pope, xxx
priesthood
    baptismal and ministerial, 5–6,
        78–87
    ontological change, 80–83
    relational change, 83
priests, 6

Rahner, Karl, xvii, xxi–xxiv, xxx
    n29, 3, 41–43, 51, 55, 94n10,
    96–97, 107, 114
Ratzinger, Joseph Cardinal, xxv,
    xxx n29, 19n5, 32, 33n28
religious life, 64–65
Rynne, Xavier, x n1

salvation, xxii–xxiv, 52, 78, 103–17
    universal, 109–17
Sanks, T. Howland, 113n13
Schloesser, Stephen, xxi n13
secularism, 44–45
Segundo, Juan Luis, 153
sensus fidei, xxv, 4, 5
signs of the times, xxi
Suenens, Léon Joseph Cardinal,
    17, 19n6, 20, 23

Taylor, Charles, xxvii–xxviii,
    131–32